LOCAL PLEASURES

Simple, sensational, seasonal cooking from the Maritime Northwest harvest

By Barbara Hazen Shaw

Think global
Eat local

CONTENTS

INTRODUCTION   4
ACKNOWLEDGEMENTS   20

SOUPS BY THE SEASON   23
   Spring Soups   25
   Chilled Soups of Summer   32
   Soups for Fall Harvest   37
   Dark Season Soups   45
   Stock Answers   62

ABOUT SALADS   64
   Salads in Spring   67
   Summer Salads   71
   Fall Salads   83
   Salads for Winter   88
   Making Salad Dressings   95

EGG DISHES   99
   Boiling Eggs   100
   Fried Egg Dishes   103
   Baking your Eggs   105
   Making Crepes   112

SEAFOOD   114
   Outdoor Seafood   114
   Stove Top Seafood   117
   Oven Baked Seafood   126
   Making Fish Stock   129

VEGETARIAN MAIN DISHES   130
   Cooking Spring Vegetables   130
   Using Summer Vegetables   134

Enjoying Fall Vegetables 144
Winter Veggie Dishes 151

ABOUT POULTRY AND MEAT 156
Cooking Poultry 158
Red Meat Dishes 166

POTATO DISHES 170
Stove Top Potato Dishes 170
Oven-baked Potato Dishes 181

VEGGIE SIDE DISHES 186
Veggies for Spring 186
Summer Vegetable Sides 191
Fine Fall Vegetable Dishes 195
Veggie Sides in Winter 203

BREAKFAST AND BRUNCH 210

CASUAL MEALS 217
Pizza from Scratch 217
Pizza Topping Ideas 219
Pita Pocket Ideas 221
Sandwich Ideas 222

FRUITS AND DESSERTS 224
Spring Fruit Treats 224
Summer Fruit Delights 226
Fall Fruit Pleasures 234
Winter Fruits 241

SUSTAINABLE OPTIONS 245
RELEVANT READING 250
QUIPS AND QUOTES 257

INTRODUCTION

This is no science tome, but a pinch of anthropology and a quarter teaspoon of history might be of interest at the outset.

Who would have guessed that cooking and the use of fire, as long ago as 1.5 million years, could be what sparked our ancestors to develop large brains, and smaller teeth and guts? Chimpanzee researcher Richard Wrangham says eating only raw food demands bigger teeth and jaws and leaves creatures too short on calories for thinking. Big human brains, like big supercomputers, require lots of energy, twenty times the energy per pound as muscle tissue at rest.

The first use of cooked food may have been when a curious Australopithicus found an animal killed by a forest fire. Or perhaps roots, fallen into a geothermal spring and fished out, tasted great. The advantages of cooking probably were discovered in many places, by different ancestors. We may never know just when early humans first cooked, but we do know that what they ate and how they acquired and then prepared it lies at the deepest roots of culture. And culture, of course, is our species' best survival tool.

In both the natural and human worlds, food habits and choices are basic to lifestyle. Ecology is largely about how various life forms find or make food in a complex, recycling pattern of give and take. Cultures center on how groups of people provide for their basic needs, food being primary.

South Asian culture is shaped by the needs of rice cultivation, for instance, as Mexico and Central America are by corn, Greece by goats and olive trees, Iowa by soy beans and pork and the dry zones of the American West, by beef, and of Australia by sheep. And everywhere on earth, including here and now, food is surrounded by tradition, myth and belief. And yet despite a cultural conservatism around what is good to eat, in the United States in recent decades eating has been revolutionized by several trends.

Easier travel, world trade and immigrant communities have brought to our shores a tsunami of new ethnic foods and new food shops. The green revolution, the spread of genetic tampering with our food supply, huge federal subsidies to agro-business makers of chemicals and tricky tactics have unnerved a lot us, convincing us to eat organic. The result, is conventional food so cheap here that a huge factory food industry grew up to add imagination, packaging and TV campaigns to simple ingredients, in order to turn a profit. Advertisers spend billions to sell us -- and our kids -- on fast food convenience, succulent artificial flavors, and fun snacks with bad stuff in them, hoping we will ignore the fine print listing ingredients we can't pronounce.

The FDA, EPA and the whole US government are protecting our food supply, right? That was the original intent of the law. But today, directors of federal agencies move back and forth between government jobs and working for the very industries they are supposed to regulate for citizens. Ever wonder why Europe, where taxes fund national health care and create a big motive for keeping populations healthy, bans so many ingredients and GMO foods that Americans are still consuming?

Many of us buy from Big Farm, without realizing the health consequences – to our families, the environment and the world economy. Millions suffer degenerative diseases while Big Pharm jumps in to save us, and children and adults go on drugs to compensate for symptoms a good diet and some outdoor play could cure.

In the same time period, technology plus economic pressures and feminist ideas have pushed or liberated women from the role of cook and maid while only the privileged get household help. All this leaves most of us wanting our meals at home to be free of harmful things and easy to be prepare, while providing maximum health and minimum damage to the fragile natural world. This book is intended to energize your move in that direction. But change is not easy.

Our personal food experiences and individual history determine how we garden, shop, cook and eat. We all have habits firmly in place, many of them from forgotten ancestors, others shaped by advertisers. And if we enjoy healthy food, and have a sense of adventure about our lives we stay open to new possibilities. Habits do die hard, but even the most risk-aversive can appreciate a good but unfamiliar meal of fresh, wholesome and well-prepared ingredients.

This book is about the possibility of returning to a focus on the basics, food grown as nature intended, close to home, harvested in its season of perfection and prepared with care and affection, for people who are important to us. It's about maximizing our pleasure with the end goal of good health, while minimizing our personal impact on a world of limited resources. It's about making a tiny dent in the 20 percent of U.S energy consumption that goes toward getting food from seeds to your table.

The facts are complex and they are not all in yet. It's difficult to figure out the best course of action. When we choose home grown or local organic, we beat all the statistics. We can't go wrong on eating if we follow Michael Pollen's simple advice... "Eat real food. Not too much. Mostly plants."

The tantalizing draw for most of us is delicious, succulent, beautiful "Slow Food" and the waning art of sharing pleasure with good people. When you grow, buy, cook and eat with friends, you create that most sought-after missing ingredient of modern life, a sense of community. And with community, we reshape culture to lifestyles that will survive and thrive in times of change.

IN DEFENSE OF THE EXOTIC

While I admire those serious Locavores who make a point of eating only what's produced within a hundred miles of home, it seems perverse to say food trade and exchange have no place in better eating. In fact, food trade is so old and so important to society that most tribal people practiced it. There's no doubt that trade in foods was ongoing in the bright morning of the earliest civilizations, and will go on until the end.

Salt lay at the core of many ancient trade routes, because everyone needed it for health and for food preservation, and not all areas supplied it. The wealthy empire of Salzburg (Salt Town) in Austria was based on this trade. Salzburg's wealth came from the 4000-year-old Celtic salt mines, in the nearby mountains, above Hallein. In the 21st century, camel caravans still carry salt 500 miles across the Sahara from the slave-labor mines of Taudenni, to Timbuktu where it heads down the Niger River to the salt trade center for West Africa, at Mopti.

Trade in food items is ancient. Arabian and African spices graced the tables of dynastic Egypt and Babylon.

In the thirteenth century, Marco Polo saw thousands of pounds of pepper from the Malabar Coast of India enter the Chinese port of Hangzhou -- each day. Wars were fought over the right to trade cinnamon and nutmeg. The entire colonial era, from Columbus in search of "The Indies" to oppression in the "Banana Republics" to twentieth century wars and independence battles were fueled by a desire for lucrative trade in and control of supplies of exotic spices and foods.

Today, the rich countries' demand for chocolate, tropical fruits, coconut, coffee, tea and other delights still distorts the farm economies of dozens of tropical countries, as small farmers are pushed off the land -- and rainforests decimated -- so profitable export crops can be grown by businesses.

On the up side, trade in recent centuries led to food exchanges between quite disparate traditions, and enrichment of everyone's food choices. The Spanish took potatoes to Europe from the Inca Empire, and for the first time Europe's peasants there could grow and cook a hearty staple that didn't require a trip through the grain mill, at a cost of up to a quarter of the crop. Spanish conquistadores carried home hot peppers, vanilla, tomatoes, quinoa, corn, chocolate and many kinds of beans from the Mayas and Aztecs. Bananas, cultivated in New Guinea and Indonesia for tens of thousands of years, have spread everywhere in the tropics.

Today, taco shops, burger stands and quick wok stir-fries serve the world daily, using local foods in new ways. In Asia, McDonald's serves rice. The tastiest food in Holland is Indonesian. Sydney has half a dozen Tex-Mex spots. Shanghai's young crowd loves Burgers, Middle Eastern, and German beer halls. In recent decades, tourism and travel may be the largest factor to alter food tastes, while the food channel on TV, the millions of recipes on the web, along with internet video phone calls, have connected us with people and food in all parts of the world. We live in a privileged time and place where we can explore much of the world. I've visited 60 countries and in each enjoyed excellent and surprising meals that broadened my culinary horizons. And the world comes to us with immigrant Jamaicans, Ethiopians, Thais, Mongolians, Peruvians, Greeks, Poles, Malaysians and more, opening good restaurants even in small towns.

One measure of a great cuisine has always been the diversity of ingredients, and the prestige associated with rarity. Ego needs are here to stay but in our day, hand crafted and organic local foods have become the status symbols once reserved for exotic nutmeg or costly chocolate. We can afford to pay the price for the best imports, but love that we have some really fantastic cheeses made close to home, and that our own wise choices make a real difference.

SUSTAINABILITY

With climate shifts affecting harvests, and the demand for bio-fuels driving up the price of food, a good look at our food system quickly reveals problems. Numbers tell a story with which no one can argue. To produce one calorie of beef with the current American system, we use 35 calories of fossil fuel. For pork, it's 68 calories in, for one calorie out. And both those figures are costs of production before adding energy required for transport, processing, packaging, marketing and storage. The average production costs for all food in the U.S. in terms of energy is twenty calories of fuel consumed for each calorie of food you eat. Nearly all of the energy input and most of the agro-chemicals come from petroleum. And then there's the push toward Cheap and Fast, a trend at the core of America's nutritionally poor foods, and another large topic.

The Green Revolution seemed miraculous as population rose and hunger fell. But that era was the great gift of cheap oil, which has allowed for the manufacture of equipment, transport of seed, mechanized plowing and planting, chemical fertilizers and pesticides. It's made us slaves to such unpleasant molecules as herbicides and their manufacture, transport and application. It has pushed pests to mutate rapidly into forms chemicals can't harm, leading to escalation of pesticide offenses. Intensive use of fossil fuels and petroleum-based agrochemicals has led to pollution of soils and water supplies, die-off of wildlife and higher rates of cancer. Pumping down of ancient aquifers for irrigation continues.

We depend on oil for the work of harvest, transport, processing, packaging, shipment and refrigeration. Worldwide, the demand for meat and other high protein food is rising with wealth, and atmospheric carbon dioxide rises causing climate alterations that affect farmers everywhere. At the same time, more marginal land is brought into production, land that will require even more energy input to stay productive. Though we may count on brilliant technology to rescue us, it doesn't take a genius to see the potential for problems ahead as the human population passes seven billion.

When the weather changes, farming practices that once worked well may be less productive. Shifting crops to another region sounds easy, but what do you do with the expensive equipment and how do farmers learn enough, fast enough to replace lifetimes of experience? Transitions take time, knowledge and investment.

More demand chasing less supply pushes prices up. It's a basic law of economics. Droughts in Australia and Argentina send wheat prices soaring worldwide. Demand for corn-based ethanol manufacture in the Midwest pushes up tortilla prices in Mexico. Demand for palm oil clear-cuts Malaysia's virgin rain forests. Freak storms hit farming areas. Rice growing nations ban exports to keep prices low at home, and their former customers go hungry. The poorest people worldwide find the price of cooking oil and other fats is forcing them to cut back. Hungry people get angry and angry people act. These facts point to a complex, energy-hungry food system that may not be as dependable as we thought.

Acquiring more of our food from nearby is one way to help assure our food future. And the wonderful part of that prescription is that food from nearby is fresher, better for the energy equation and the environment, and better for our health. Additional positives include the satisfaction of growing some of our own, getting to know local products and producers and reconnecting with the sources of what sustains us, all leading to a richer experience of life.

HERE AND NOW

Food from our own gardens is the ultimate in eating local. Home grown requires nothing more than a little attention to detail – learning about plants and soil preparation, digging in the compost and manure, then buying seeds or starts in spring and remembering to water them during our dry summers. Anyone with a sunny spot can raise some fine produce, even if it's in containers on a deck, or a few squash plants in the flower beds.

Growing food is a powerful experience for kids. When I pulled a radish from our kindergarten yard, grown from a seed we'd planted a few weeks earlier, it was a high point of my first five years – a miracle right up there with my first tricycle.

Do teach children about gardens, but don't pressure yourself if you're no farmer. Good, healthy food can be as simple as shopping with care for natural ingredients and treating them with respect and a modicum of skill. Of course, it can be a real challenge to wean people from a habit of unhealthy packaged foods, snacks full of hydrogenated fats, preservative chemicals, high fructose corn syrup and sugar substitutes. These manufactured substances are created by people intimately familiar with the demands of our psyche and stomachs for what was rare and special to our wild ancestors. It's hard to resist them, because they are designed to be VERY hard to resist. Shopping differently is key. Will it be bags of nachos, or sliced vegetables and fruit?

It's often said that shopping for health is a stroll around the perimeter of the grocery store, where the fresh items reside, avoiding the long aisles of boxed, bagged and canned items heavily advertised. The added benefit of perimeter shopping is saving money. For example, a stop in the bulk food aisle for a pound of organic oats at, 95 cents, delivers more value than a 16-ounce box of sweet oat cereal flakes sold at four or five times the price.

So, are you ready to toss those empty calories on your shelves? Probably not. Rather than toss edibles, just let "food-like substances" run out, then don't buy any more.

I had to explain to my kids that to be the best parent I know how to be, to do my most important job, I have to provide the best food I can. It took several tries to get across the idea that my goal was for them to grow stronger and smarter, and look fabulous, while preserving the planet. If that argument doesn't sell the idea, a kid's got problems.

And it's not easy. Instincts rule when hunger gnaws. If the family craves snacks, be ready in advance with colorful, tempting alternatives in pretty dishes, front and center in the refrigerator. A friend lost a lot of weight, and has kept if off, just by changing her snack habits and always having fresh veggie sticks ready, to meet the munchies with great ammunition.

Old paradigms change slowly. The transition from the common American diet to really good food can be a challenge for a nation and for an individual, but it is one you and I can manage. I go through periods of intense interest in improving my food awareness, then go along at that level until another inspiration occurs. I've still got a long way to go.

The path from my kind of simple good local organic eating to sensuous, fabulous local gourmet organic cuisine, is a long road. It takes talent, experience and probably a very refined teacher to get to the top. Only a select few want to go there. You know if you are on that road.

In both growing and cooking for the best outcome, I'm in the middle -- no beginner, but far from professional. I'm an amateur, in the original sense of the word, one who does it for love. I learned from a self-taught mother, aunts, sisters and talented pals, plus lots of books. I worked for a San Francisco executive chef with 48 cooks, and made tarts with a Swiss pastry chef. I enjoy cooking demos and classes and spent a few days at Cordon Bleu classes in Paris. Hardly enough, but worthwhile indeed.

I cooked for forest workers, for the small crew of a Caribbean freighter and for lots of parties at home. One of my best inspirations has been my son who spends half a day making a meal from the French Laundry Cookbook. I keep learning, but I'm no chef. I know it's chemistry and physics, and I did study those. But I love cooking because it's magic, a secret alchemy anyone can practice, to transmute earthy ingredients into luxurious golden pleasures.

THE KITCHEN

Beginners' kitchen guides and how-to books are incredibly helpful for anyone starting out, explaining what you need to set yourself up – staples and spices to have on hand, techniques, tools and even measuring. A good kitchen supply shop is a treat to explore, tempting cooks with gorgeous and useful purchases, while magazine photos of extravagant kitchens thrill the decorator in all of us.

But quality of food has little relationship to equipment, despite the claims of those with something to sell -- unless, of course, you cook for a living. In China, we made great meals on two propane burners, with one wok, one saucepan and one steamer. In Mexico, we buy great fresh produce right off the farm in the marketplace, but cook on two burners with pathetic pans.

My own kitchen includes dishes on open shelves, a large hanging pot rack, a bottom-freezer refrigerator and an ancient freezer in the garage. I also have a pantry cabinet on the back porch. My big indulgence is a fancy smooth-top electric range that has cycles for food drying and bread proofing. That kind of wizardry seems pretty amazing to a gal who cooked several years at an 1891 wood-burning cook stove, up in the hills south of Dufur.

I'd love to cook with gas, but gas pipes don't serve our area. So, I make do with electricity. We have basic pots and fry pans of various sizes, and I am partial to cast iron. We have a drawer full of hand tools, plus blender, food processor, a mixer wand, and a little coffee grinder perfect for nuts and grains. I reject single purpose tools (except in the hands of the working professional who actually needs them daily). We keep all the basic ingredients on hand and a huge variety of spices and herbs, in case of inspiration.

ABOUT THE RECIPES

All recipes serve four, unless otherwise specified.

Though the recipes provided may call for spices and salt and olive oil, the shopping and cooking ideas I share with you focus primarily on local products -- fruits and vegetables, staples, dairy, eggs, meat and seafood produced here by conscientious professionals. Exotic, imported or rare ingredients show up only occasionally and in small amounts. Maybe that's cheating, but it simplifies everything to have access to spices and good olive oils we can't grow locally. Yet. My goal is not to prove you can eat totally local, but to inspire home cooks with a great variety of creative ways to turn more and better local foods into delectable meals.

The recipes emphasize flavor and simplicity. Basic kitchen savvy, but no culinary academy expertise, is required. I repeat: all recipes serve four, unless otherwise specified. Divide or multiply quantities if you choose. Standard U.S. measures are used.

MEASURING

TB means tablespoon, equal to 3 tsp or teaspoons.
Four TB equals 1/4 cup.
A cup is an eight-ounce measuring cup.
All temperatures are Fahrenheit.

I apologize to the rest of the world that the U.S. has not switched to vastly simpler metric system, like everyone else. And the British system of weighing everything seems silly when you can dip up a cupful with the same result.

Early cookbooks seldom included quantities. Recipes before the late 1800s called for a handful of this and a pinch of that. The adoption of consistent measurement surely helped the amateur cook do a decent job of it. But the kitchen is not the chemistry lab or we'd see recipes calling for 5.607 grams of cilantro and 3.098 grams of salt. When quantities come out even, recipes are in reality approximating.

So relax about precision until you are cooking in a restaurant where consistency is vital. Besides, in the real world, products of nature vary tremendously. How different one peach can be from the next. And many food items closely resemble each other, either in effect or taste, so are naturals for substitution. Thus, many of these recipes offer a number of optional ingredients.

Cooking is at its best when it's creative self-expression. Cook with friends and children. Have a good time. Try an occasional challenge, like using a power saw to cut into a huge winter squash. Go on a weekend cooking binge. Try new crops and products. Sniff and sample, make a field trip to a farm, visit an ethnic market, add lots more spices. In our own kitchens, experimenting is a great way to learn. Cook with spontaneity. Taste often. Play with your food.

Good home cooking demands experience. The best way to get experience is to make some mistakes and figure out what you did wrong. How else can you discover the limits of reality, but by testing them, as children naturally do? Luckily, we can compost our worst and still get an "A" in the dining room.

AUTHOR'S POINT OF VIEW

I'm a home gardener and food preserver, but I do a lot of food shopping for the basics as well as for local artisan foods made with care, and I appreciate excellent nutrition. I love to forage for wild foods and to harvest a succulent salad in a meadow, or just outside the back door.

I like to try making things most people simply buy, like ricotta, mayonnaise and crackers. I'm curious about anything I don't understand, about food origins and how foods are made and those obscure foreign words for good things. I enjoy cooking and sharing tasty meals based on what I grow, but haven't the savoir faire to pretend I'm a serious gourmet. Or maybe my sense of smell is only average. Not that I don't enjoy indulging in the very best. But hard-core purist, I'm not.

With a career that included laboratory research, various aspects of energy conservation, science writing and managing an energy information center, current energy issues are a large concern of mine. With an M.S. in physiology, and a lot of reading plus a bout with cancer behind me, I'm convinced organic is important. The low-cost American food supply is built on non-sustainable practices that degrade natural resources and we'll probably find out in few decades that the system doesn't do our health all the good Nature intended.

We can't go on doing what we are doing now. The U.S. puts over four million tons (yes -- 8,000,000,000 pounds) of pesticide and herbicide into the environment each year, and over 20,000 different chemicals. These include hundreds of powerful and long-lived antibiotics and pharmaceuticals, many of which accumulate in our bodies -- and in the bodies of every other species -- plant, animal or microorganism. We have very little data on the long-term outcome of exposure to these chemicals, or the effects of exposure to several at once. But evidence is mounting that the costs may turn out to be far higher than we thought.

New data point to environmental poisons as a factor in the accelerating rates of autism in our children, low sperm counts in our young men and more birth defects, not to mention cancers later in life. Any reduction of those numbers will boost our health and that of the ecosystems that support all life.

Growing some, buying some from local producers, shopping with care, becoming intimate with nearby resources, living close to the earth in one special place, we can transform our lives and turn our region's bounty into wonderful eating. That is the beginning of a quiet revolution we can lead from home.

Organic foods taste better, cost more and will keep you and your children healthier with far higher "nutrient density." But sometimes conventional is what's available. I encourage everyone to support sustainable agriculture and ecosystems upon which our lives depend, but to shun food snobbery.

It's about being in balance with your world. And it's about a growing appreciation for these miraculous bodies we inhabit, evolved to live in a world without man-made chemical complexes and thus, terribly and unpredictably vulnerable to accumulation of trillions of these molecules in our environment and our own tissues.

Embracing these truths, let us give the best we have to our children, because we dare to dream for each one a long good lifetime as we watch them today, growing their fragile brains and bodies with the nurture we provide. Embracing our own best interests, let us stay vigorous into old age as we say yes to health and abundance for all, yes to good food from the good earth of our farms and gardens and the good fields and waters of home. Let us embrace 'Biophilia' and hold in our hearts the web of deep connections that bind us all to our land, to our foods and to each other. May we feel love and respect for the accumulated experience and care, the daily work and the knowledge that supports our own good lives.

ACKNOWLEDGMENTS

This collection borrows concepts and ingredients from brilliant chefs and media mavens. Much came from family and friends. I offer special thanks to all who delighted me with surprising flavors and shared their secrets.

Famous food experts give generously of inspiration but only a few of them focus on great ideas for eating locally, though I expect that is quickly changing. With a few notable excep-tions, even those who love our unique bioregion use plenty of un-seasonal foods from far, far away.

Alice Waters of Chez Panisse in Berkeley is an exception, in California. She teaches about the elegant and healthful possibilities close to home. She is a pioneer of the local food movement and one of my heroes. A visit to her edible schoolyard project in Berkeley, watching middle school students prepare and eat the food they grew, helped me realize this is an idea whose time has come.

And now, my deep and heart-felt thanks to the hundreds of friends, instructors and acquaintances who helped me evolve my food awareness. Thanks to Mu for rhubarb and Du for planting all those great fruit trees, to Mama for pies and Daddy for great breakfasts and that steak house in Rialto. Thanks to Charles and Evelyn Greenwood and Charlie and Linda, and to Gertrude Lovejoy on Lopez Island. Thanks to David Barnes who taught took me to the gamekeeper's house outside Paris, to Genghis' family in Ankara and the Mukhlos family in Baghdad. Thanks to Tino O'Brien who ate my omelets in Beirut and to the policemen who made us fresh fish for breakfast in Adana. Thanks to Bob

Schechter who got mad enough to make me rethink a few things about my cooking. Thanks to Chef Kenneth Juran in San Francisco who let me watch, and to Captain Manny of the Wendy B who insisted I feed the crew with whatever he had on board.

Thanks to Chris Hazen and his dad, grandma and great-grandpa—each of whom taught me a few food tricks. Thanks to Carol Jackson and Kay Kammerzell on San Juan Island for wonderful oysters and wine in the woods. For moments of inspiration, thanks to Dawn Presta, now in Idaho, to Alice and Galyn in Eugene, to Allan Johnson in Seattle.

Thanks to Lynda Bush who showed her impatience and made me want to do better, then took me to her favorite DC area restaurants. Thanks to Cindy Chan and her brothers Colin, Clement and Chris for generous hospitality in Hong Kong. Thanks to Sigga in Paris, the Mingos in Livingston and the Graves in Missoula for wonderful food experiences.

Thanks to the whole Henderson clan for entertaining talk and hearty mid-west fare in Iowa and Nebraska. Thanks to Dick in Napa, Nate and Lynn in Berkeley, Megan and Rick in San Francisco -- all for excellent evenings with food. Thanks to John and Lois for great appetizers made by daughter Rachel, and for introducing me to Ethiopian food. Thanks to Dana for the best Mexican in the L.A. area. Thanks to Mary for my first Jamaican. Thanks to Paula Kruse for letting me do a few things in the Tahoe kitchen and to Dave Kruse who made me eat a whole raw fish in Utrecht. Thanks to Bob Johnston who always insisted on doing dining right and made sure I was included for a dinner that was the best meal of my life, in Amiens.

A huge "Thank you" to authors mentioned in the reading list, for contributing to my ongoing education, and for offering knowledge, attitude and wisdom. I am grateful to each of you for the great ideas I've gleaned from your pages and modified to focus on Northwest ingredients, after some simplifying in my own kitchen. I wish I could meet each one of you to tell you how glad I am for all you have contributed to my own life and to enriching our world.

SOUPS BY THE SEASON

EARLY SPRING can be a slow time for harvesting, but young greens that love the cool rain pop up early and last until warm weather sets in. The winter dangers, aside from very low temperatures, are wind and rain damage that toughen plants. Some gardeners and many vegetable farmers use plastic greenhouse covers.

My winter and early spring staples from the garden include arugula, kale, chard, kohlrabi, rutabaga, beets, calendula, sorrel, dandelion and parsley. All are planted in fall. In years that I grow leeks, they winter over too. By late winter the only roots that are not too woody are a few beets and kohlrabi. But by March any of those left behind are putting up new, tender shoots. We always leave old, gnarly kale plants too, because in spring they produce a huge crop of tender young flower buds that resemble broccoli, long before any broccoli is ready. Kale buds are a popular crop at April farmers' markets too.

For those who like to toss things together and invent soups, a good rule is that an amount of water or stock to just cover chunked vegetables will make a soup that is neither too watery nor too thick. If you add grain or pasta, add extra water as they soak up lots.

A delicious pureed soup can be made from just about any combination of vegetables. Add salt and pepper, plus herbs. Add cream to transform this humble pleasure into a sumptuous gourmet event. If you want fewer calories, without loss of richness, substitute evaporated milk. Or use a veg stock and go vegan.

An easy way to puree is to use a submersible mixer wand, rather than transfer everything to a blender or food processor. The wand leaves a soup with more texture than one pureed smooth in a blender. If you must have a refined puree, never fill a blender more than 2/3 full of hot soup. Hold the lid down with a towel as you gradually increase the speed. Boiling greens releases most of the flavor and nutrients into the water, not a problem for soups, but it's why many recipes call for wilting greens by tossing with oil.

To salt a soup like a pro, remove a small scoop from the pot and taste it. Add a bit of salt. Note which flavors now seem more distinct, how many of the ingredients you can identify. Add more salt. Is it better, or not? When you reach an ideal point, challenge your taste memory to remember that level of saltiness. Return the bit to the pot and start adding salt to the main batch. Add until you get to that correct point you remember.

Spring Soups

SPRING GREENS AND CHEESE SOUP

Use any combination of spinach, arugula, turnip, collards, mustard, lettuce, chard, beet tops, kale, parsnip greens, dandelion or calendula leaves, etc. The yellow cheese can be jack, mozzarella, Edam, havarti, etc.

1 pound chopped mixed greens
3 cloves garlic, minced
3 TB butter
3 TB flour
2 cups stock
1/2 tsp each: paprika, nutmeg, thyme
Salt and pepper to taste
2 cups milk, buttermilk, or sour cream
Garnish:
1 cup grated yellow cheese

Grate the cheese and set it aside for garnish. In a large fry pan, melt butter and saute' garlic. Add greens and tumble them until they are well wilted. Sprinkle flour over greens and mix again. This will help thicken the soup. Add stock, spices, salt and pepper. Use a mixer wand or transfer to a blender to puree. In the original pan, simmer soup five minutes. Remove from heat, add milk or cream and mix well. Re-warm but do not boil. Serve hot, topped with the grated cheese, nicely melting. Croutons optional.

EGG & SORREL SOUP (French POTAGE GERMINY)

French sorrel is a sour-tasting leafy plant that comes back each year, tolerates neglect and can be easily propagated from roots that spread. Leaves, available here all year, add tang to any green salad and many soups. Tiny leaves of wild sorrel can also be used, but harvesting them is tedious. Watercress is a tasty alternative to sorrel.

In summer and early fall, purslane can be used in this recipe. Some see purslane as a marginal, low-growing weed, but it was the favorite vegetable of Mahatma Gandhi. Portulaca oleracea, common purslane, known as Verdolaga in Italy, contains more Omega-3 fatty acids than any other leafy plant and is sold in markets near the Mediterranean. Only with sorrel is the soup a real Potage Germiny.

2 cups washed, packed sorrel leaves
3 TB butter
4 cups stock
1 cup milk
2 beaten eggs
Salt and pepper to taste
   Garnish: Sprigs of fresh chervil

In a large pan, melt butter and stir in leaves, tumbling them as they wilt. Add stock. Simmer two minutes. Remove from heat. Stir in beaten eggs, salt and pepper, then milk. Mix well and reheat to serve. Sprinkle with chervil. Herbed croutons are optional.

HOT AND SOUR RADISH SOUP

I like hot and sour soup a bit spicier than this recipe. Add more cayenne if you like. Hot and sour is a Chinese invention. The soup is very quick to make.

4 cups stock
1/4 cup rice vinegar
2 TB sugar
1/4 tsp each: ginger powder, cayenne pepper
1 pound raw shrimp -- peel and de-vein
1-1/2 cups sliced radishes or daikon
1-1/2 cups chopped spinach or chard
1/2 cup chopped green onions

In a large pot over medium heat, bring to a boil a mix of vinegar, sugar, cayenne and ginger. Add shrimp and simmer about 4 minutes. Turn off heat, stir in radishes, spinach and green onions. Cover and let stand 3 minutes before serving.

EMERALD ISLE SOUP

Spring mustard greens and spinach give this soup its gorgeous color.

5 green onions, chopped
4 garlic cloves, minced
4 TB butter
2 TB flour
4 cups stock
1 cup cream
1 tsp cider vinegar
1 tsp each: cayenne, nutmeg
6 cups chopped spinach, packed
1 cup chopped mustard greens, packed

Over medium heat, saute' onion and garlic in butter four minutes. Sprinkle in the flour and cook another minute while stirring. Slowly add stock as the soup thickens. Add remaining ingredients slowly. Bring to a boil and cook five minutes more. Cool slightly, then puree with an immersion wand blender.

SPRING ONION SOUP

Quick and easy, this soup is good with a grilled cheese sandwich for a light meal.

12 to 15 green onions, minced
3 TB butter
3 TB flour
2 cups stock or salted water
3 cups milk or half and half
Salt and pepper to taste
   Garnish: Fresh chopped chives

In a large pot, over medium heat, saute onions in butter 2 minutes. Blend in flour to make a paste. Slowly add stock or water as the mixture thickens. Continue simmering until onions are tender, about 6 minutes. Just before serving, add milk, salt and pepper. Re-warm but do not boil.

ICELANDIC PEA SOUP

Hearty *Saltkjot og baunir* was eaten on Shrove Tuesday in Iceland, to fill up on meat before Lent. It's best made the night before, so flavors can meld.

1/2 cup dry split peas
4 cups water or stock
1 tsp salt
2 strips bacon, chopped
1 pound lamb or ham, cubed
1 tsp dry thyme
2 chopped carrots
1 rutabaga, peeled and diced
1 medium potato, scrubbed and diced
Salt and pepper to taste

In a large pot, simmer dry peas in salted water 40 minutes. In a fry pan, saute bacon and lamb or ham until meat is lightly browned. To the peas, add meats and all other ingredients. Simmer one hour. Thanks to Barb Gilmour for testing and improving this recipe, great with lots of lamb.

SPRING CHICKEN SOUP

This is similar to a soup developed by the Food Network Kitchens. Use fresh herbs if available.

2 cups chopped cooked chicken meat
4 cups chicken stock
4 chopped scallions
2 chopped medium carrots
2 TB each: fresh chopped parsley, tarragon
1 bay leaf, 3 long strips lemon peel (zest)
1 bunch asparagus, cut to 1-inch
1 cup edible pod peas
7 sliced small mushrooms

In a large saucepan, simmer chicken and stock with the onion, carrot, herbs, bay, and lemon zest about 20 minutes. When ready to serve, add the asparagus, peas, and mushrooms. Cook another 5 minutes. Remove the bay leaf and strips of zest. Serve hot.

VERMONT SPRING SOUP

This recipe makes a dish similar to an old Yankee favorite, The peppery flavor comes from fresh watercress. Find a similar taste in bright yellow wild spring mustard flowers.

3 TB butter or oil
2 scallions, chopped
2 cloves garlic, minced
1 small turnip, peeled and chopped
2 medium red potatoes, diced
2 medium carrots, chopped
1/2 tsp dried thyme
1/2 cup fresh parsley, minced
6 cups stock
1/2 pound asparagus, cut to 1 inch
1 cup peas, fresh or frozen
1 bunch (6 ounces) watercress, chopped
2 TB vinegar
Salt and pepper to taste

Melt butter in a fry pan over medium heat and sauté scallions, garlic, turnips, potatoes, and carrots two minutes. Cover and cook over low heart until vegetables start to soften, about 5 minutes. Transfer this to a deeper pot. Stir in thyme, parsley, and stock and simmer 15 minutes more. Add asparagus and peas and cook another 5 minutes.

Purée half the soup with all the watercress and return it to the pot, leaving some chunks for texture. Stir in vinegar, salt and pepper. Serve hot. Thanks to Barb and Frank, for feedback that improved this recipe.

PORTUGUESE SPRING GREENS SOUP

Use early wild mustard greens, tender turnip greens, kale or broccoli rabe for this nourishing and distinctive soup.

1/4 cup olive oil
1 onion, thin sliced
3 cloves garlic, minced
1/4 pound spicy sausage
4 cups water or stock
2 medium gold or white potatoes, diced
Salt and cayenne pepper to taste
3 cups chopped, packed greens

Start potatoes in their own pot and cook until soft, then drain and mash them. While the potatoes cook, in a heavy pot, saute' onion and garlic in oil. Add sausage and fry two or three minutes. Add stock or water, the mashed potatoes, salt and hot pepper to taste, then cover and simmer 30 minutes. Add chopped greens and cook another five minutes.

FRENCH SPRING POTATO SOUP

3 TB butter
1 leek, chopped
2 cloves garlic, minced
2 cups each: water, stock
6 small potatoes, chopped
6 small young carrots, thin sliced
1/4 cup dry white rice (or barley)
1/2 tsp minced fresh rosemary
2 tsp salt
1 bunch of fresh spinach, chopped
1/2 cup heavy cream (or half and half)

In a fry pan, over medium heat, cook leeks and garlic in butter until tender. Add them to a large pot of stock, water, potatoes, carrots, grain, rosemary and salt.

Simmer 30 minutes, until vegetables and grain are tender. Stir in chopped spinach and heavy cream. Re-warm and serve hot.

Chilled Soups of Summer

Since assigned a story on cold summer soups, when writing for the Bend Bulletin, I've collected lots of recipes for these summer season pleasures. Cold soups from a number of traditions are perfect for hot days. Russian borscht, French Vichysoisse, white bean soup, Polish cucumber soup and Spanish Gaspacho are some of the better-known possibilities. In Scandinavia, summer is the season for chilled fruit soups.

COOL WHITE GASPACHO

In Spain cooks use almonds in the gazpacho, but tasty filberts grow in our region.

1 pound toasted, skinned filberts
1/4 cup olive oil
3 cloves garlic
1 TB white vinegar
3 cups stock
Salt to taste
3/4 cup diced day-old heavy white bread
    Garnish: 1/3 cup crushed filberts

In a blender, puree skinned filberts and oil until very smooth. Add other ingredients except garnish nuts, and puree again. Serve cold, topped with a sprinkling of crushed filberts. To toast raw filberts, or any raw nut, bake on a cookie sheet at 250 for 40 to 45 minutes. More if needed.

CUCUMBER AND SMOKED SALMON SOUP

This soup is excellent with small cooked shrimp, instead of smoked salmon. Sour cream or buttermilk instead of yogurt yields a similar result.

2 medium cucumbers
1 cup plain yogurt
1 cup stock
1 tsp each: dry chives, chervil, parsley
Salt and a dash of hot sauce, to taste
8 oz. smoked salmon
    Garnish: 1/2 peeled and diced cucumber OR Chopped fresh parsley OR a spoonful of fresh red salsa

Peel, seed and dice the cucumbers. Puree the cucumbers with yogurt, herbs, salt and hot sauce. Serve cold, into bowls. Break up fish into half-inch pieces and scatter into each bowl. Serve cold, topped with your chosen garnish.

COLD CUCUMBER WALNUT SOUP

Lemon cucumbers are especially easy to grow in the maritime northwest, but many types thrive here. Just plant them in late May, water them in dry weather and stand back. Oven at 350F

1 cup walnut meats
4 medium cucumbers
1/2 cup chopped green onions
1-1/2 cup whole milk plain yogurt
3 TB warm honey
2 TB minced fresh dill
Salt to taste
    Garnish: 1/4 cup of the roasted walnuts.

Roast walnuts in 350F oven for 15 minutes, cool and chop them. Reserve 1/4 cup for topping. Peel, seed and chop the cucumbers then puree half the cucumbers and 3/4 cup of walnuts with yogurt, honey and salt. Stir in other ingredients. Mix well. Top with reserved walnuts. Serve cold.

LYNDA'S CUCUMBER SOUP

My sister's chilled summer soup is always a big hit. She uses a preparation called *Better Than Bouillion*, available in better groceries, instead of stock. A soup almost as good can be made with three zucchinis.

3 large cucumbers, peeled and chunked
1 large onion, peeled and diced
2 Tb butter
6 cups stock
1 tsp dill
1 tsp white pepper, salt if needed

Simmer cucumbers about 10 minutes. Saute onion in butter until soft. Combine everything and puree. Serve chilled or warm.

CHILLED BEET SOUP

This is one of the few beet soups I've found not based on the famous Russian borscht. Use two cups apple juice if you don't have unsweetened cranberry on hand.

1 large (3") red, golden or white beet
1 cup apple juice
1 cup unsweetened cranberry juice
1/2 cup plain yogurt
4 TB vegetable oil
Salt to taste, plus a dash of hot sauce
    Garnish: Fresh mint

Simmer the whole beet 20 minutes, then peel and chop it. Mix and puree all ingredients. Chill in the refrigerator one hour. Serve into bowls. Garnish each bowl with bright green mint leaves.

CHILLED ARUGULA SOUP

Arugula planted in fall will produce tasty leaves from late winter until almost summer. Plant it in early spring for a crop in early summer.

5 chopped green onions
2 packed cups chopped arugula
1/2 cup, loosely packed fresh basil
1 red bell pepper, chopped
2 cucumbers, peeled, seeded and chopped
2 cups plain yogurt
2 TB each: olive oil, warm honey
3 TB cider vinegar
Hot sauce to taste

Into a blender put one cup of yogurt, all the onions, basil and arugula and half the bell pepper and cucumber. Puree, then add the honey, vinegar and olive oil. Pulse again to mix. Pour into a large container and mix in the remaining chopped pepper, cucumber and yogurt. Serve chilled.

COLD TOMATO AND GARLIC SOUP

In the Spanish tradition, this cold soup is simple, tangy and quick to make. It is best if chilled before serving.

2 pounds (6 medium) fresh tomatoes
2 cloves garlic
2 cups chopped dry bread or crumbs
1/2 cup olive oil
1/2 tsp sugar
Salt and pepper to taste
    Garnish: 2 hard-boiled eggs, sliced thin plus
2 ounces thin sliced ham such as prosciutto, in strips

In a blender, puree tomatoes and garlic. Add olive oil, sugar, salt and pepper, and blend again. Add olive oil then bread or crumbs and blend until smooth. Chill the soup. Garnish each bowl with crumbled egg and strips of ham.

CHILLED ZUCCHINI SOUP

If you grow even one zucchini plant, there's a good chance you may have so much you'll need creative ways to use it. This soup is a good answer.

1 chopped medium onion
3 TB olive oil
6 chopped medium zucchini
3 cups stock
1 tsp dry dill weed, or 3 tsp fresh
Salt and pepper to taste
   Garnish: Croutons, or a dollop of sour cream

Sauté onion in oil, about five minutes. Add other ingredients, cover and simmer about 8 minutes or until zucchini is soft. Puree the soup. Chill and serve with garnish.

Soups for Fall Harvest

Fall soups utilize ingredients abundant at harvest time, many of them originally grown in southern Europe and other warm regions.

FRANK'S CORN AND CHICKEN SOUP

Thanks to Frank Ratti and Barb Gilmour for this winner that Frank developed. Barb says, "Technically, it's not a chowder (no milk or cream) but it's nice and rich. I think it might be interesting to serve it with salsa and sour cream. Try substituting cilantro for the parsley."

1 carrot
1 stalk celery
1/2 large sweet onion
1 clove garlic
3 TB olive oil
3 TB minced fresh parsley
3 chicken sausages
6 cups chicken stock
1 chopped red pepper
3 cups fresh or 16-ounce bag of frozen corn
Salt and pepper to taste

Finely chop carrot, celery, onion and garlic. Over medium heat, sauté carrot and celery in the olive oil until they start to soften. Add the onion and garlic, then the parsley.

In another pan, brown the chicken sausages. (Chicken breasts or thighs would work too.) Cut meat into chunks and add to softened vegetables. Add chopped red pepper and corn, salt and pepper. Simmer until peppers are soft. Excellent with toasted sourdough bread.

TOMATO BASIL SOUP

This soup is good hot or cold. In winter, use 1 large can of tomatoes, and 4 TB dry basil.

2 pounds fresh tomatoes
1 stalk celery with leaves
1 cup packed fresh basil
1 small onion
3 minced cloves garlic
1 tsp minced jalapeno pepper
6 TB butter
2 TB each: balsamic vinegar, honey, Worcestershire sauce
2 cups stock
1/2 cup dry white wine
1 tsp each chopped thyme, oregano
Salt to taste
   Garnish: A dollop of plain yogurt or heavy cream OR tiny basil leaves and flower petals.

Chop the tomatoes, celery, basil and onion. For a more refined soup, sieve out the tomato skins and seeds. Over low heat, saute' garlic and onion in butter until translucent. Add other ingredients and simmer about 5 minutes. Puree about half and return it to the soup. Nice with scattered tiny basil leaves and petals of basil flowers.

ITALIAN VEGETABLE SOUP

Incredibly rich and satisfying, this soup is easy to make. Add butter if your stock is low in fat. It will provide a good "mouth feel" as they say in the trade. This recipe makes enough that the soup can be your main course.

2 cups cooked white beans
6 cups stock
1 cup each chopped: celery, carrot, onions
2 cups each chopped: savoy cabbage, kale,
2 cups cubed sour dough bread
4 cups chopped tomatoes
1/2 cup chopped fresh basil
1/4 cup olive oil
6 minced cloves garlic, salt and pepper to taste

Chop the vegetables and cube the bread. Puree half the beans to thicken the soup. Combine all in a large pot. Simmer 20 minutes. Serve hot.

TOMATO AND CORN SOUP

Bred and grown by early people in Meso-America, corn and tomatoes seem made for each other.

3 cups chopped fresh or canned tomatoes
1 cup fresh, canned or frozen corn kernels
3 TB butter
3 cups stock
1 tsp each: dry thyme and rosemary, sugar
Salt and pepper to taste
    Garnish: Grated sharp cheddar cheese

Add all but the cheese to a big pot, then simmer for 15 minutes. Serve hot, topped with grated cheese.

CORN AND TOMATO BISQUE

This garden soup is good warm or cold. Bisque is a thick, creamy, well-seasoned soup of French origin. It was originally made from lobster, crab, shrimp, crayfish, or various vegetables. Try small frozen shrimp in this version.

2 cups fresh or frozen corn kernels
1 cup chopped tomatoes
1/2 cup grated carrot
1/2 cup grated potato
1/2 cup chopped onion
4 TB butter
3 cups stock
2 cups buttermilk
1 tsp. fresh minced thyme
1/2 tsp. each: nutmeg, dry mustard and sage
1 TB honey
Salt and cayenne pepper to taste

Over medium heat, saute onion in butter. In a large pot, combine onion with other ingredients. Simmer 15 minutes. Puree half and return to the pot. Serve hot with crackers.

GARDEN MINESTRONE

Add tofu, tempeh, mushrooms or chicken for a variant on this flexible soup. The vegetables can be tomatoes, peas, green beans, broccoli, summer squash, turnip, kale, chard, peppers, celery, etc. Choose two or three from these fresh herbs: parsley, basil, marjoram, chervil, lovage, oregano, thyme, garlic, rosemary.

2 cups cooked white beans
3 cups chopped fresh garden vegetables
1 chopped small onion or leek
1/4 cup olive oil
4 cups stock
1 cup bowtie or spiral pasta
4 TB fresh herbs
Salt and pepper to taste

Toss it all in a big pot and simmer about 30 minutes. Serve hot. Great with quesadillas or hot buttered corn bread.

FRUIT AND VEGETABLE SOUP

1 tart apple, diced
10 Brussels sprouts, quartered
1 chopped onion, thin sliced
6 cloves garlic, sliced
1 fennel bulb, thin sliced
2 cups apple juice
2 cups stock
1 TB minced fresh rosemary
1 TB minced fresh marjoram
Salt and pepper to taste

Prepare apple and vegetables. Combine all ingredients in a large pot and simmer 30 minutes. Adjust the salt and pepper. Serve hot.

ZUCCHINI DILL SOUP

4 TB olive oil
1 cup chopped onion
3 garlic cloves, minced
5 zucchinis, 7 or 8 inch long
2 TB fresh dill
4 cups stock
Salt and a dash of hot sauce to taste
    Garnish: Fresh basil and sour cream

Slice the zucchini and prepare onions and garlic. Sauté onion, garlic and zucchini in oil until tender. Add stock. Simmer 5 minutes. Puree half and return it to the pot. Serve warm or chilled, with garnish.

APROVECHO TOMATO SOUP

When you have too many tomatoes, chop and freeze some in baggies and you'll have a good supply on hand after the weather turns cold. Tomatoes are simple to can, too, or use purchased products. Try fresh, canned or frozen tomatoes in this recipe from Rosy at the Aprovecho Sustainability Education Center, west of Cottage Grove, Oregon.

1/2 stick butter
2 chopped bell peppers
1 chopped onion
5 minced cloves garlic
10 chopped tomatoes (1 large can)
1/2 cup brown rice
2 cups fresh milk
1 cup water or stock
Salt and cayenne pepper to taste
    Garnish: Grated sharp cheddar, or other cheese

In a large pot, over medium heat, melt the butter and sauté peppers, onion and garlic. Add tomatoes and cook them until mushy. Add rice, milk, water, salt and hot pepper, then cover and simmer over low heat one hour. Serve hot, garnished with grated cheese. Lovely with fresh baked bread or rolls.

AUTUMN WATERCRESS SOUP

Look for watercress, a member of the mustard and arugula family, growing along clean grassy meadow streams. Cook it to kill waterborne organisms. It likes wet roots and plenty of sunshine. You can also find it in better produce departments.

2 cups packed watercress
2 TB butter
3 diced medium potatoes
5 cups stock
1 TB parsley
Salt and pepper to taste

Trim and chop watercress then in a fry pan, sauté until it wilts. Set it aside. Cook the diced potatoes in the stock with parsley, salt and pepper for about 20 minutes or until potatoes are soft. Add the watercress and the puree to soup, leaving some chunkiness.

Dark Season Soups

Soups for late fall and winter are hot and hearty, made from roots happily buried beneath the chilly earth, plus preserved foods of all kinds, combined to cook up the perfect warm filling meal for a dark and stormy night. Served with crusty bread, cheeses and a hot drink, soup is the center-piece of some of our favorite meals. Pureed soups are great with croutons.

To make your own croutons, sauté bread cubes in oil or butter to which savory herbs and spices have been added, until they begin to brown. Sauted croutons won't sink like baked ones will.

ISLE OF SKYE CARROT SOUP

Claire MacDonald served this buttery carrot soup at her Kinloch Lodge on Scotland's Isle of Skye. A variant calls for a thumb-sized piece of fresh peeled ginger, sliced thin and tossed in.

1/2 stick butter (4 TB)
1 cup chopped onion
5 cups chopped carrots
1 cup peeled and chopped potato
4 cups stock
2 tsp coriander
Salt and pepper to taste
    Garnish: Minced fresh parsley

In a big pot, slowly cook onions in butter, then add other ingredients. Simmer 45 minutes. Puree and serve hot, topped with parsley.

POTATO BROCCOLI SOUP

This basic soup comes in many versions. Most kids like its gentle flavors.

2 medium onions, sliced thin
3 TB each: olive oil, butter
3 cloves garlic, minced
3 cups chopped broccoli
3 cups diced red or Yukon gold potatoes
2 cups stock
Salt and pepper to taste
    Garnish: 1/2 cup fresh grated Parmesan

Slowly cook onions in oil and butter until soft. Add garlic near the end. Put these in a big pot with other ingredients. Simmer 30 minutes. Serve hot, each bowl topped with fresh grated Parmesan.

VEGETABLE CHOWDER

1 bell pepper, seeded and chopped
1 chopped onion
2 sliced carrots
1/4 cup olive oil
2 cups fresh or frozen corn kernels
2 chopped potatoes
1 small can tomatoes
1 tsp thyme
Salt and pepper to taste
2 cups each: milk, stock
1/2 cup fresh basil leaves

Over medium heat, sauté carrots, onion and pepper in oil. Add corn, potatoes, tomatoes, stock, thyme, salt and pepper. Simmer 30 minutes. At the end, add milk and basil. Re-warm to serve. Add chicken, shrimp or shellfish if you wish. Or put a pat of butter in each bowl to melt.

OYSTER CHOWDER

Near Campbell River, on Vancouver Island, we first picked up wild oysters on the beach. Most grocery stores now sell jars of fresh-shucked oysters, too. If you like them raw, you get huge doses of vital B-12.

4 slices bacon, chopped
1 onion, chopped
1 leek, white part, chopped
1 medium fennel bulb, thin sliced
4 cups stock
2 cups chopped potatoes
1 bay leaf
1 tsp each: thyme, salt, white pepper
1 cup oysters, shelled
2 cups half and half
1 TB fresh grated lemon zest

Sauté the bacon in a large pot, until it's almost crisp, then remove the pieces. In the bacon fat, sauté onion, leek and fennel until they soften. In a large pot simmer stock, potatoes, bay, thyme, salt and white pepper for 20 minutes. Add the bacon pieces, oysters, half-and-half and lemon zest. Simmer 5 minutes more. Add salt if needed.

CREAMED VEGETABLE SOUP

Infinitely variable, here's a good way to make fine use of stored veggies on hand, and to experiment with herbs you like. Add cream to nearly any combination of vegetables in soup -- delicious. Other vegetables to use: carrots, turnips, parsnips, broccoli, kale, kohlrabi, white beets, cauliflower, winter squash.

1 cup chopped onion, leak or shallot
1/4 stick salted butter
3 cups stock
1 tsp honey
1 cup chopped potatoes
2 cups other chopped vegetables
Fresh garden herbs
Salt and pepper to taste
1/2 cup heavy cream

Slowly cook onion in butter until it's soft. In a large pot add this to all the other ingredients, except cream. Simmer 40 minutes. Remove from heat and add cream. Puree all, part or none depending on preferred texture. Serve hot. To create a hearty soup, add a can of cooked white, black or pinto beans. Adapt to your preferences.

BARLEY, BEANS AND GREENS

The greens can be dandelion, spinach, chard, bok choi, kale, collards, beet tops, etc.

1 cup diced onion
1 cup thin-sliced carrot
1/4 cup olive oil
3 cups chopped greens
13 oz can chopped tomatoes
13 oz can white or brown beans
1/2 cup pearl barley
4 cups water or stock
Salt and pepper to taste

In a soup pot, sauté onion and carrots in oil until onions are soft. Add greens and turn them until they wilt. Add beans, tomatoes, barley, water or stock, salt and pepper. Simmer about 40 minutes. Serve hot. OK to make a day ahead, or keep it several days in the refrigerator.

WINTER MULLIGATAWNY

Invented by the British, during the Raj period when they colonized India, the name means "pepper broth" in Tamil. Tamils use coconut milk, not cream.

1 each, chopped: apple, carrot, small onion
2 chopped large chard leaves with stems
1/4 cup canola oil
2 TB flour
4 cups stock
1 13-oz can chopped tomatoes
1/2 cup each: dry rice, dry lentils
1 cup chopped tofu or chicken
3 TB curry powder
Salt and hot red pepper flakes to taste.
1/2 cup cream – added after cooking

Peel, core and chop the apple. In a large pot over medium heat, saute' onion, carrot, chard and apple in the oil until soft. Mix in the flour, to serve as a thickener. Add stock, rice, lentils, then the tofu or chicken, curry and salt. Simmer 40 minutes. Remove from heat and add cream. Serve hot.

BABUSHKA'S BORSCHT

Hundreds of Slavic beet and potato borscht variations exist. I like this one hot, with lots of sour cream. Borscht makes a fine, hearty meal served with dark rye bread and apple sauce. In hot weather, it's wonderful cold. Shocking beet-colors exit the body the next day. Babushka is Grandma.

1 large beet
2 TB butter
1 medium onion, chopped
1 carrot, sliced
1 cup canned tomatoes
1 medium potato, chopped
1 cup chopped cabbage or kale
4 cups stock
1 tsp. dill weed
2 TB cider vinegar
Salt to taste
    Garnish: Sour cream, parsley

Simmer the trimmed beet 20 minutes then set it aside to cool. In a large pot, saute carrot in oil until soft. Slide skin off the beet and chop it. Add onion and cooked beet and continue sautéing until onion is soft. Add tomatoes, cabbage, stock, dill, vinegar and salt. Simmer until all vegetables are soft. Puree. Serve hot, garnished with sour cream and parsley.

LEEK AND POTATO SOUP   (POTAGE PARMENTIER)

This hearty French country soup is very similar to *Vichysoisse*, which is frequently served cold. Another version of leek and potato soup includes a cup of chopped mustard greens in spring. If you don't have leeks, use onions, but the flavor will be a bit different. Whole milk plain yogurt can substitute for sour cream, but if you use it add a little butter for best results.

1-1/2 cups chopped white part of leeks
3 cups chopped potatoes
5 cups stock or water
Salt and white pepper to taste
1/2 cup sour cream
Garnish: Sprinkle of paprika, parsley or chives

Simmer chopped leeks and potatoes in salted water or stock about 35 minutes, or until soft. Remove from the heat and puree. Add salt and white pepper. Stir in sour cream or yogurt just before serving. Reheat but don't boil. Garnish each bowl with parsley or chives and a sprinkling of paprika.

WELSH LEEK SOUP

The Welsh raised sheep and traditionally made their leek soup (Cawl Mamgu) with lamb neck bones, removed before serving. The leek is the national symbol of Wales.

4 medium leeks including some green part
2 large onions, quartered
3 carrots, chopped
2 parsnips, peeled and chopped
1 pound lamb chunks
or 3 pounds lamb neck bones
1 TB cider vinegar
1/2 cup rice
Salt and pepper to taste
   Garnish: 1/2 cup minced fresh parsley

Clean and chop leeks. In a big pot, combine all but the parsley and simmer two hours. If you used bones, remove them, cool and clean off the meat and return it to the soup. Serve hot, each bowl sprinkled with minced parsley.

BACON AND POTATO SOUP

1/2 pound thick-sliced bacon
1 medium onion, chopped
5 cups diced potatoes
5 cups stock
2 tsp dried dill weed
3 TB dried parsley
1 cup milk
Salt and pepper to taste

Cut bacon into one-inch pieces. In a big pot, sauté bacon until it curls, then add onion and reduce heat. Cook onion in bacon fat until it's soft. Add potatoes and stock, dill and parsley. Cover and simmer 30 minutes. Remove from heat and add milk, then salt and pepper to taste. Serve hot

CARIBBEAN PUMPKIN SOUP

Alice Tallmadge brought this lip-smacking soup to a potluck and opened my mind to the savory possibilities of pumpkin. Use one large can of pumpkin. Or bake or microwave part of a large Halloween pumpkin or winter squash until it's soft and easy to remove from the shell.

4 cups soft pumpkin
2 chopped onions
1 cup chopped tomatoes or tomato sauce
3 cloves garlic
1/2 cup dry white wine
1 TB each: honey, cinnamon, white pepper, paprika, marjoram
2 bay leaves
Salt and hot sauce to taste
Garnish: 1/2 cup cream and fresh parsley

If you start with an uncooked pumpkin, soften it in the oven or microwave then peel, seed and remove the fibrous material. Put everything but the cream and parsley in a large pot. Simmer 40 minutes. Remove bay leaves. Puree the soup. Add cream and mix well. Serve hot, garnished with parsley.

PLUM TASTY PUMPKIN SOUP

Luckily for pumpkin eaters, these "fruits" not only keep for months, but are amenable to the creation of a vast variety of good foods, from pudding to stew. Dried plums (prunes) add a succulent sweetness to this soup.

2 leeks, chopped white part only
1 tsp each: sage, rosemary, thyme
1/4 cup olive oil
4 cups cooked pumpkin or winter squash
4 cups stock
1/4 cup red wine
1 cup seeded and chopped dried plums
1 cup buttermilk or yogurt
Salt and pepper to taste

Sauté leeks and herbs in oil. Add pumpkin and stock. Simmer 20 minutes, then puree. Add chopped plums, salt, pepper, and buttermilk. Reheat and serve.

SQUASH AND APPLE SOUP

Acorn, butternut or any orange colored winter squash (of which dozens of varieties exist) works in this soup. Options: make a delicious soup substituting potatoes for squash, and using a garnish of grated sharp cheddar. Try either version with 3 TB curry powder, instead of the other spices.

2 cups cooked squash, or one large can
3 cups stock
2 tart apples, cored and chopped
1/2 cup chopped onion
1 cup natural unsweetened apple juice
3 TB cider vinegar

Salt and hot sauce to taste
1/2 tsp each: coriander, thyme, nutmeg
    Garnish: Plain yogurt, fresh strands of dried chives

Combine all but the garnish and simmer about 15 minutes. Puree and reheat. Serve hot with a dollop of yogurt and chopped chives or basil.

ROASTED SQUASH SOUP

Oven at 375 F

1/4 cup olive oil
2 medium acorn squash
2 ripe pears – core and peel
2 chunked medium parsnips or carrots
2 cups stock
1/2 tsp each: cumin, ginger, dry mustard
Salt and pepper to taste
1 diced onion
    Garnish: Plain yogurt or sour cream

Halve and remove seeds from squash. Oil a cookie sheet. Place squash halves face down and roast in hot oven 30 minutes. Remove from oven and add pears and parsnips to cookie sheet. Return cookie sheet to the oven for 20 minutes more. Remove again. Cool and spoon meat out of squash.

In a large pot, combine stock, squash meat, pears and parsnips. Simmer 5 minutes. Puree this. Saute onion in oil and add to the puree. Add seasonings. Serve hot, a dollop of yogurt or sour cream in each bowl.

PUMPKIN SHRIMP BISQUE

One magazine claimed that fashion designer Oscar de la Renta invented this soup. Use shrimp shells or a handful of tiny dried Asian shrimp to make a rich broth.

1 pound shrimp in shells
1/4 cup olive oil
3 cups stock
1/2 cup dry white wine
1 medium onion, chopped
3 bay leaves
2 tsp minced fresh sage leaves
2 TB lemon juice
2 cups cooked (or canned) pumpkin puree
1 cup half-and-half milk
Salt and pepper to taste.

Peel shrimp and save the shells to flavor stock. Over high heat, sauté shrimp shells in 2 TB oil until they are browned. Add stock, wine, onion, sage, bay and lemon juice. Cover and simmer 30 minutes to create a flavorful broth. While the stock cooks, sauté the shrimp meat and sage leaves in 2 TB oil. Now, back to the broth. Cool it and strain out solids. To this add shrimp, pumpkin puree and cream. Mix well, then heat but do not boil. Serve hot.

WINTER ROOT SOUP

1 large onion or 2 large leeks
1 each: rutabaga, turnip, parsnip, carrot, potato
6 cups stock
1 TB minced fresh rosemary
Salt and pepper to taste

Trim, peel and chunk vegetables. In a large pot, simmer them with stock and rosemary about 30 minutes.

MUSHROOM AND HAZELNUT SOUP

I use a coffee grinder to pulverize nuts. Filberts are called hazelnuts in some parts of the country.

3 cups sliced mushrooms
1 chopped large onion
3 TB butter
3 TB flour
4 cups stock
1 bay leaf
1/2 tsp each: nutmeg, dry ginger, celery seeds
1 tsp each: thyme, basil, oregano
2/3 cup roasted pulverized filberts
1 cup half-and-half
Salt and pepper to taste

Sauté mushrooms and onion in butter about five minutes. Mix in flour and slowly add stock as soup thickens. Add bay leaf, herbs and spices. Simmer 30 minutes. Take out bay leaf. Remove from heat and add pulverized nuts (I use a coffee grinder) and milk, salt and pepper. Mix well. Re-warm and serve hot.

CARROT SOUP WITH CIDER

5 cups chopped carrots
1/4 stick butter
1/2 cup chopped onion
1 cup apple cider
1 tsp each: honey, minced fresh sage
3 cups stock
Salt and pepper to taste
    Garnish: Sour cream and minced parsley

Sauté carrots and onion in butter until the onion softens. Add cider, honey, stock, parsley, sage, salt and pepper. Simmer 20 minutes. Puree and serve hot, with a dollop of sour cream in each bowl, and a sprinkling of parsley.

WILD RICE AND MUSHROOM SOUP

Native Americans, who harvest true wild rice in canoes, look down on the domesticated item. The Willamette Valley now has several rice growers who cultivate dark rice, sold as "wild." You can use dry *shitaki* mushrooms, but soak them an hour in warm water first. Save the flavorful soaking water for stock.

1/2 cup wild rice
6 cups stock
2 cups sliced fresh mushrooms
2 TB olive oil
1 cup eachchopped: onion, carrot, shitake mushrooms
3 TB soy sauce
1 TB minced fresh parsley
Salt and pepper to taste
1 cup heavy cream

Cook wild rice in one cup of the stock about 45 minutes or until tender. Sauté fresh or soaked mushrooms, plus onion and carrot in the olive oil until onions are soft. Put all ingredients, except cream, into a large pot and simmer together ten minutes. Remove from heat and add cream. Serve hot

MUSHROOM SOUP WITH DUMPLINGS

This soup is good with wild or purchased mushrooms.

    Soup:
2 cups mushrooms -- cleaned and sliced
3 TB butter
2 TB soy sauce (or tamari)
3 TB flour
4 cups stock
    Dumplings:
1 cup flour
1 tsp baking powder
1/2 tsp salt
3 TB dry chives
3/4 cup stock as the liquid

Sauté mushrooms in butter, add soy sauce, mix in flour. Slowly add stock as the soup thickens. Keep soup hot while you mix up the dumplings.

In a mixing bowl, combine all dumpling ingredients. Form dough balls about an inch in diameter and spoon them into the hot soup. Cover, simmer soup 10 minutes.

WINTER CARROT SOUP

The Marche' Restaurant in Eugene served a group of us a carrot soup so glorious, I had to try making it at home. This soup is now one of my personal favorites. Another version uses none of these spices, instead calling for 1 tsp each, thyme and dill, plus 2 TB hot sauce. The fresher and sweeter the carrots, the better the soup.

6 cups chopped carrots
1 cup chopped onion
4 cups stock
2 TB each: olive oil, butter, honey
1 tsp each: ginger, cinnamon, cardamom, mustard powder, white pepper, rosemary
1/2 cup red wine (or apple juice)
1 cup half-and-half milk
    Garnish: Chopped chives or fresh mint

Simmer all but the milk for about 30 minutes or until carrots are soft. Puree, then add the milk. Rewarm. Serve hot, garnished with chopped chives or mint.

DANISH APPLE SOUP

Apple soup is easy, tasty, satisfying and uses ingredients we usually have on hand -- except maybe the cream. You can use applesauce, or fresh apples.

1/2 stick butter
1 cup chopped onions
3 peeled and diced tart apples
3 cups stock
1 cup cream
Salt and pepper to taste

Saute onions and apples in butter until soft, about 7 minutes. Add stock, cream, salt and pepper. Simmer about 15 minutes. Serve hot.

WINTER CURRIED PARSNIP SOUP

Long-time gardeners know that parsnips are sweetest if dug up after the first frost. You can use rutabagas instead. This soup is easy, hearty and filling, with a yummy texture.

3 cups peeled and chopped parsnips
1/2 cup chopped onion
3 cups stock
2 TB butter
1/2 cup chopped, cored and peeled apple
2 cloves garlic, minced
1 tsp. each: dry thyme, rosemary, pepper.
1 TB curry powder
1 lime's juice
1/2 tsp salt, or to taste
1 cup milk

Into a large pot, put all but the milk. Cover and simmer 25 minutes or until vegetables are soft. Puree about half the volume. An immersion wand blender is the perfect tool. Reheat and add milk just before serving. Tested and made more delicious by Ellen Singer, who suggests making a double batch so you have plenty for later.

Stock Answers

Stock is the foundation for delicious, nourishing soups and sauces. Conventional canned stocks and broths usually contain MSG, and are very high in salt. If you use them, look for low sodium organic, and don't add more salt to the recipe. Or, make your own rich and satisfying stock, using roasted bones, leftover meats or only veggies.

Most encyclopedic cookbooks discuss stock making at length. Generally, the recipes call for roasting bones and meat scraps at 450 degrees until they just brown. This brings out the natural flavors before you toss them in the stockpot. Save all bones in the freezer until you accumulate a supply. Roasted or not, simmer them in water with a bit of acid such as a little vinegar or lemon juice to dissolve out the calcium and other important nutrients in bones. Cook on low heat for many hours. You can feed soft bones to pets.

Victoria Schneider makes a lot of bone broths. She says, "The secret is using lots of knuckle bones for the gelatin-rich cartilage." Schneider also uses marrow bones, and may throw in a bag of rib bones and T-bones from the freezer. "We bag and freeze bones whenever we have some left over after dinner. I don't bother to put vegetables into my stock at this time, knowing I will put lots into the soup. I simply roast the bones, then fill a large stock pot with as many bones as it will hold, fill it with water and a few tablespoons of vinegar to help pull minerals into the water, and then leave it at a low simmer for well over two days." Two days! (all weekend) Yes, on very low heat. Or use a pressure cooker, hissing for a couple of hours.

For fish stocks, use mostly non-oily fish, carcasses plus heads with gills removed. Use trimmings but not tails (bitter) -- no innards and no roasting. White wine is good in fish stocks. For a quick and tasty fish stock, keep on hand a bag of smelly Asian dried shrimp, with eight times the Vitamin D of liver and loads of iodine. The odor quickly departs with simmering, leaving nutrients so important to health that dried shrimp is a major ingredient in the food of even the poorest, in Africa. Strain to save the succulent broth and give solids to pets or to the compost.

Veggie stocks are delicious too. Leftover bits of vegetable, their skins, saved cooking water, remains of gravy, leftovers and much more are all fair game for the stock pot. Add only small amounts of strong tastes such as artichoke, turnips, asparagus, carrot tops, broccoli or cabbage. Avoid incompatible elements, including dry peas and beans. Add delicate greens like spinach only at the end. Don't use old or flavorless veggies. Gourmets inform us that with soup stock, as with computer programming, Garbage In Garbage Out.

All stocks need garlic and onions. Tomato and celery are core ingredients for meat stocks, but not absolutely required. Adding an assortment of herbs produces a richer product. Many cooks use a bouquet garni, a little tied cloth bag of herbs, is simmered in the stock then easily discarded. In Eastern Europe, they use dried parsnip tops - very tasty. Parsley, peppercorns, thyme, oregano and a pinch of nutmeg all enliven a good stock. Black pepper, and dried or fresh mushrooms intensify flavor because they contain glutamates, natural versions of the taste stimulators in mono-sodium glutamate (MSG).

French cooks like a stock with a mix of chopped aromatics called a mirepoix, made from carrots, onion, leek and celery, simmered long then put through a fine strainer. Some cooks add corncobs, seaweeds, dried veggies, or foraged finds. Add enough water to cover, then simmer slowly for at least two or three hours, adding water as needed. Or, with the vent fan on, let the water boil off to reduce the stock so flavors will concentrate and intensify. Strain the stock to remove solids.

If you save stock in the refrigerator, boil it after three days, to sterilize it again. Store the stock for a week or two in the fridge, boiling every three days. Better yet, freeze it for later in small amounts for convenient thawing. Pour only cooled foods into plastic, to minimize chemical reaction products migrating into the food. If you freeze in glass, leave an inch at the top for the expansion of ice crystals. When using stock for soup, if the soup tastes flat try adding salt plus fat such as olive oil or butter. If it tastes a bit bitter, add a little something sour plus some honey. Experiment with herbs and spices too, and you may save an otherwise dull brew.

ABOUT SALADS

Who doesn't love a salad in summer, made from crunchy lettuce and greens and fresh tomatoes, or a luscious mix of juicy fresh fruit? As the weather cools, we enjoy the last of the hot weather crops.

Gorgeous nuts, apples and pears are ready in October. But fresh produce is one thing novice "locavores" might imagine we'd be deprived of in winter. Not so. In our mild climate, local crops can keep us supplied. So can our gardens, if we plan things right.

In the US, 70% of the lettuce comes from California, most of it iceberg. Americans consume over three billion heads a year. It's shipped all over the country in refrigerated rail cars and trucks -- big agro-business indeed. The main reason we originally invited migrants over the border was to do the exhausting "stoop labor" required to weed and harvest this demanding and fragile crop that's served as salad in every café in the country, twelve months out of twelve.

Since the era of the old time café and Mom's lettuce and tomato toss, salads in our country have grown far more creative. Arugula, raddichio and mache' entered our vocabularies and our kitchens. Grated carrots and red cabbage add color to winter's greens. Berries and sliced fruit add piquant flavor. Pickled or tasty fermented vegetables and crisp sliced roots to dip into sauce add variety to our fresh fare. We gaze at pictures in food magazines, savoring gorgeous salad ideas from the most talented artists of food photography.

A colorful winter salad platter of local foods can include slices of red onion or purple cabbage, palest green kohlrabi and bright carrot strips, sliced pickles, nuts and slices of cheese. It's a feast for the eyes and keeps us feeling good.

Can we really make it through a winter without foods from far, far away? Yes. When imagination ranges beyond buying whatever fresh vegetable, or exotic fruit catches our fancy, we rediscover the joy of seasonal eating all year from our own gardens and nearby farms. The selection is, naturally, limited. And we can have a wonderful variety of tasty, healthful food, as fresh as it gets. Vegetables 20 minutes out of the earth make a far better salad than food that's traveled a thousand miles, even if that means no fresh tomatoes or cucumbers in January.

To grow your own winter greens, plant in late summer. Kale, chard, arugula, mustard, collards and bok choi will all make it through to spring. Root crops like beets, carrots, turnips, potatoes and even kohlrabi will be there into January but, after that, some become woody. For spring greens, prepare soil in late winter. A sunny, fertile 4 x 8 foot area is more than enough to supply a mix of lettuces for a family. Sow lettuce seeds in February for a harvest beginning in May.

A clear cover, of glass or plastic, to protect baby plants minimizes damage from rain and hail and also conserves warmth from the sun, so they grow faster. Do allow for air circulation to prevent mold. Keep the cover in place until the greens need more space. By that time the weather has improved, too. Sow greens every few weeks for continued production into July. In August or September, pull up any stragglers, add soil amendments and sow arugula and other hardy varieties for harvest through the winter.

Edible flowers have come into vogue again and dress up any salad. Rosemary, basil and lavender blossoms add subtlety to a salad of spinach or mixed greens. Nasturtium leaves and flowers, calendula and marigold petals, dianthus, violet and viola (Johnny jump up) flowers add color and good taste. Use rose petals in fruit salads. Asians have long loved steamed or stir fried buds of common day lilies, and the young leaves are tasty in March and April, too. In April, if you know where to find a rich lavender-blue camus meadow, pick leaves and flower buds as tender vegetables.

Before I serve friends anything as odd as flowers, I try some myself. If it's good, I next try a little positive marketing, let them know I've made something rare and special for them to get them in the mood for a new experience. Earlier failures to do that resulted in rude responses when the surprise hit. "Hey, this stuff is not lettuce."

Salads in Spring

SIMPLE SPRING SALADS

To create a healthful, simple salad for four, buy a half-pound of mesclun (Mes KLOON). This is a mix of baby greens, in Provence traditionally at least a dozen varieties -- for the 12 apostles. Or pick a mix of greens from the garden. The greens themselves provide an exciting variety of tastes. Try adding colorful early spring blossoms -- calendula petals, violets, pansies or violas. Nuts, cheese, tofu cubes, meat, shrimp or fish, and other enrichments can turn a green salad into a meal. Dress greens just before serving, since they loose color and crispness quickly in the presence of oily and sour flavorings. Serve with hearty breads.

SNOW PEAS AND MINT

Later in the season, make a salad very similar to this one with fresh cucumber slices, instead of snow peas.

1 pound whole edible-pod peas
1/2 cup chopped onion
1/4 cup chopped fresh mint
1 cup plain yogurt
1/2 tsp cumin
Salt and pepper to taste
Fresh leafy greens

Steam peas and chopped onion about two minutes. Or put them in a large strainer and dip to blanch in boiling water 30 seconds. The idea is that they should be barely cooked. Drop them into cold water to instantly halt cooking. Toss with other ingredients. Serve on a bed of fresh leafy greens.

FIDDLEHEAD FERN SALAD

Out in the woods in May, or April at lower altitudes, you'll discover the bracken ferns are sprouting, and their tender green curls unfurling. Rub off the brown fuzz and taste the sweet almond flavor. Sometimes fiddleheads show up in the better stores, but most that are picked fly to big cities for use by top chefs, like the one I worked for in San Francisco. Strange as it seems, we find fiddleheads from far across the country in our markets. Thanks to chef Beau Vestal for this recipe.

20 fresh fiddleheads, each 4 to 5 inches
4 green onions, chopped
4 cups tender young greens
1/3 cup olive oil
1/2 cup white wine
Salt and pepper to taste

Arrange greens on four salad plates. Over medium heat, sauté onions in oil one minute. Add fiddleheads and toss one minute more. Add salt and pepper. Remove from pan and cool three minutes, then lay them on the greens. To the fry pan, add wine. Heat to dissolve and scrape up juices sticking to the pan. Divide warm juice over the salads.

FIDDLEHEADS AND MUSHROOMS

The serious Northwest forager can enjoy this elegant dish modified from a New York Times recipe, made from the best stuff in our woods. Local mycological society field trips are your best guide to learning about local wild fungi. Never eat a mushroom you can't positively identify.

2 TB butter
2 cups sliced fresh mushrooms
2 cups fern fiddleheads, cleaned
1/2 cup chopped walnuts
Balsamic vinaigrette
Salt and pepper to taste
    Garnish: Shaved aged Parmesan

Sauté mushrooms in butter about five minutes, then cool. Have a bowl of cold water ready. Boil a pot of water and drop fiddleheads in to simmer one minute. Lift out with a slotted spoon, and put in cold water to halt cooking. In a bowl, toss mushrooms and drained fiddleheads with walnuts, dressing, salt and pepper. Garnish with Parmesan cheese.

SPRING RADDISH SALAD

In Poland, they make a salad very similar to this one from grated kohlrabi, and another from grated fresh young beets, with a pinch of nutmeg.

Start with a bed of young greens on each salad plate. Add to each about 1/3 cup grated fresh radishes and some thin sliced onions. Dress with a nice balsamic, or make a dressing of oil, vinegar, sugar and salt.

WATERCRESS SALAD

You can add other vegetables to this salad. If you gather wild watercress, be aware that most streams contain a gut parasite called Giardia. Pick only cress parts that are well above the water. Soak them at least in hour in cold water to which you have added a teaspoon of chlorine bleach, per gallon. Then rinse cress well before using. Farmed cress is safe.

1 bunch watercress
4 green onions, chopped
1/2 cup radishes, thin sliced
1/2 cup mushrooms, thin sliced
Vinaigrette dressing

Carefully wash and clean the watercress. Use only the leaves, saving the thicker stems for stock. Toss with other ingredients and dressing.

BRAISED LEEK SALAD
Oven at 350F

1/2 cup olive oil
1/2 cup white wine
1/2 cup white wine vinegar
1 tsp each: celery seeds, thyme, ground mustard, salt
4 large leeks
3 hard cooked eggs
3 cups young greens
Salt and pepper to taste

In an ovenproof fry pan, heat a marinade mix of oil, wine and vinegar with spices and salt. Trim tough tops from leeks and split each one into quarters, the long way. Clean out any dirt. Lay leeks in the marinade mix and place the pan in the hot oven for twenty minutes.

While leeks cook, boil the eggs ten minutes, cool, peel and slice them. Set aside. Cool the leeks and chill them an hour. Just before serving, divide greens onto four salad plates. Dress them with some of the marinade mix. Divide leeks onto the salad plates and top with sliced eggs, salt and pepper.

Summer Salads

By July or early August, warm season crops are producing an abundance of the produce we wait for all year. And then we find ourselves with a vast overabundance.

SIMPLE SUMMER SALAD

Create a bed of fresh greens for each diner. Add sliced cucumber, fresh seedless grapes, walnuts. Around edges lay thin slices of fruit in season, such as cherries, apricots, plums, peaches or apples, or others at peak ripeness as summer progresses.

TOMATO AND GREEN BEAN SALAD

I discovered this combination one August, when the garden gave us loads of tomatoes and green beans at same time. This salad is quite filling and makes a good main dish for a summer lunch outdoors.

1 pound green beans
4 juicy ripe large tomatoes
1/2 red onion, thin sliced
2 cloves garlic, minced
Balsamic vinaigrette dressing
    Garnish: Crumbled feta cheese, Fresh parsley sprigs, 1/2 cup toasted sunflower seeds

Clean, trim and cut beans into two-inch lengths. Steam beans 4 minutes, then plunge into cold water to halt cooking. Chop tomatoes and slice onions. Toss vegetables with seeds and dressing. Serve onto salad plates and top with feta crumbles and parsley.

FRESH CORN SALAD

When fresh corn season has passed, this salad is good with frozen or canned corn. I've made it as a hot dish in winter.

2 cups corn kernels
2 cups chopped tomatoes
1/2 cup thin sliced red onion
1/2 cup chopped fresh basil
1/2 cup crumbled feta cheese

Place chopped onion in a large strainer, dip it into boiling water for 30 seconds, then cool under tap water, to soften the flavor. Cook fresh corn, then use a knife to scrape kernels off the cob. Mix all ingredients together with 1/3 cup balsamic vinaigrette dressing. Serve cold.

GREEK SALAD

4 ripe tomatoes
1 large peeled cucumber
1 green bell pepper
4 oz crumbled feta cheese
2 tsp dill weed
1/4 cup olive oil
Salt and pepper to taste
Optional: kalimata olives on the side.

Trim, then slice or chop vegetables and toss everything together.

STUFFED TOMATOES

At the height of their season, choose plump vine ripened tomatoes still warm from the sunshine. Leave the stems on. Slice off he top quarter of each fruit. Scoop out the contents.

Fill with a mix of tuna or salmon and sour cream, seasoned with salt and fresh herbs. Or fill with a mix of rice and feta with herbs. Serve at room temperature, with their tops on.

GRATED ZUCCHINI SALAD

3 small (6 -7") zucchinis
2 medium tomatoes
2 TB minced fresh mint
2 TB dried chives
3 TB olive oil
2 TB cider vinegar
Salt and pepper to taste

Clean and coarsely grate zucchini. Quarter tomatoes and remove seeds and juice. In a salad bowl, toss vegetables with other ingredients. Chill one hour. Serve cold.

ZUCCHINI CARPACCIO

2 zucchini, 7 to 9 inches
1 tsp salt
2 cups chopped packed arugula
1/3 cup coarsely grated Parmesan
2 tablespoons extra-virgin olive oil
1/4 teaspoon black pepper

Thin slice zucchini then toss with 3/4 tsp of the salt. Let it drain in a colander for 15 to 20 minutes, then using a dishtowel gently squeeze out any liquid.

In a salad bowl, toss arugula with remaining salt, plus half the Parmesan, oil and pepper. Arrange zucchini slices on the arugula and drizzle them with remaining ingredients. Serve chilled.

SICILIAN SUMMER SALAD

Chopped or sliced hard salami makes an authentic addition to this Mediterranean favorite.

2 medium white potatoes diced
1 cup green beans cut to two inches
3 chopped ripe tomatoes
1 medium cucumber
1/4 cup olive oil
3 TB vinegar
Salt and pepper to taste
    Garnish: Black olives, sliced salami

Simmer potatoes and green beans until al dente, just cooked. Peel cucumbers and slice them thin. Chill cooked potatoes and green beans. Toss with other ingredients. Garnish with black olives and salami.

GARDEN GASPACHO

In Spain, it's gazpacho and can be either a soup pureed in the blender or a salad, both made with the same summer vegetables and some bread. You can omit croutons and add soft bread chunks to absorb vegetable juices.

3 cups chopped tomatoes
1 cup cucumber
1 cup sliced zucchini
1/2 cup chopped bell pepper
1/4 cup chopped onion
2 TB wine vinegar
3 cloves garlic, minced
1 TB each: lemon juice, olive oil
    Garnish: Garlic croutons

Peel, seed and chop the cucumber and prepare other vegetables. In a large bowl, combine all ingredients and mix well. Refrigerate several hours. Serve with crunchy croutons.

TURKISH SUMMER SALAD

2 diced tomatoes
1 diced bell pepper
1 diced onion
1/2 cup minced parsley
4 mint leaves, minced
4 TB olive oil
3 TB cider vinegar
Salt and pepper to taste

Prepare vegetables and stir all together. Chill 20 minutes, so flavors blend. Great in pita pocket with feta cheese, or dipped on big chips.

SPINACH AND NASTURTIUMS

Nasturtiums bloom from June through the first freeze, if planted in late February. The tender leaves and blossoms add a peppery bite and exotic look to this simple spinach salad. Spinach wins kudos for high vitamin levels, and its abundant calcium, magnesium, iron and antioxidant flavinoids. But it can be tricky to grow here, since it bolts to seed stalks at the first hint of heat.

3 cups young spinach, packed
2 cups nasturtium leaves and flowers
2 hard-boiled eggs
1/2 cup chopped walnuts
Balsamic vinaigrette dressing
Optional: 1 tsp chopped fresh tarragon leaves

Wash and dry the leaves and flowers. Peel and chop hard cooked eggs. Roast walnuts in a 350F oven for 15 minutes to bring out their best flavors. Cool them. Toss together with the dressing and serve at once.

FIG EXTRAVAGANZA

8 very ripe perfect figs
4 oz chunk of Gorgonzola or Bleu cheese
Prosciutto ham slices
16 walnut halves (optional)

Cut each fig in half the long way. Press into the center of each half a chunk of cheese 1/2 to 3/4 inch. You may add one walnut half atop the cheese. Or not. Wrap each morsel in a strip of prosciutto. Place them on a baking sheet. Broil about 2 minutes or until cheese starts to melt, but not longer. Serve warm with wine. The same concepts work very well for stuffed apricots, peaches or nectarines. Cut in half, press bleu cheese into the center, sprinkle with nuts. Omit the prosciutto. Or not. Serve warm or cold.

YOUNTVILLE FIGS

The French Laundry Restaurant in Yountville, in the Napa Valley served this warm fig dish. Six halved figs go in a large frying pan with one TB olive oil, one thin sliced shallot, one bay leaf and a 4-inch sprig of rosemary. Cook over medium heat while shaking the pan, for 5 minutes. Pop into the oven at 450F for five minutes. Remove, and arrange figs on a platter. Discard the rosemary and bay leaf. Add 1 TB balsamic vinegar to the cooking pan and stir to pick up flavors. Drizzle this sauce over the hot figs.

GREEN SALAD WITH FIGS

When fig season is past, make this salad with thin sliced apples and pears.

3 packed cups salad greens
8 ripe figs
4 oz aged goat cheese
1/4 cup Balsamic vinaigrette dressing
Garnish: edible flowers

Toss greens with dressing and divide onto four plates. Stem and halve the figs. Arrange figs or other fruit around the greens, a chunk of goat cheese beside them. Scatter bright flowers such as calendula or nasturtium over the salad.

WALDORF SALAD

Waldorf salad dates to 1896, when it was an immediate hit at New York's Waldorf-Astoria Hotel. For variety, use chopped dates or soaked (to soften) dry fruits instead of raisins. Or include cubes of leftover cold chicken, turkey or pork to make the salad a main dish -- great for lunch with warm bread.

2 tart apples, cored and diced
1 cup chopped celery
1 cup seedless grapes
1/2 cup raisins
1/2 cup walnut meats
2 cups greens
    Dressing:
1/4 cup mayonnaise
1/4 cup plain yogurt
1 TB apple juice
1 tsp dry mustard

Mix dressing. Toss it with all but the greens. Lay each plate with a bed of greens then top the greens with the salad and dressing mix.

VIENNESE CUCUMBERS

2 medium cucumbers
1 TB salt
3 green onion, chopped
3 TB wine vinegar
1 TB warm honey
6 TB canola oil
Salt and pepper to taste

Remove about half the cucumber skin by running a peeler down the length of it. If seeds are large or hard, remove them with a spoon. Slice thin. Toss slices with 1 TB salt. Mix up the remaining ingredients as dressing and toss cucumber slices with it.

CUCUMBER RAITA (RYE ee ta)

Popular in India and all over south Asia, I first tried this easy favorite on the train to Calcutta. My friend Arun Toke' says there are dozens of variations on the raita theme. His favorite includes lots of fresh cilantro. Popular variants add sliced red onion, chopped mint and a dash of hot cayenne pepper. Other people add chopped tomatoes, red bell pepper and celery. We start with the most basic version.

3 cups cucumber
1 cup plain yogurt
1 tsp cumin
Salt and pepper to taste

Peel and seed cucumbers, then slice or chop. Spread chunks on a dry cotton towel for ten minutes to remove some of the water. Then mix them with yogurt, cumin, pepper and salt.

TOMATO BASIL RAITA

This raita doesn't even use cucumbers.

1 cup yogurt
2 chopped tomatoes
1/3 cup packed chopped basil leaves
3 TB olive oil
Salt to taste

Stir tomatoes and basil into yogurt, then drizzle olive oil over the top. Add salt.

GREEK PURSLANE SALAD

Purslane is a lowly weed to some, while in Italy and Greece it is a valued vegetable. It's happy in poor soil, with little water but demands plenty of sunshine. It's loaded with nutrients. In our area, it's at its peak in late summer, on dry sunny ground.

2 medium tomatoes
1 medium onion
1 medium cucumber
1 green pepper
1 cup purslane
2/3 cup crumbled feta cheese
1/4 cup olive oil
2 TB cider vinegar
2 TB minced fresh oregano or marjoram
Salt and pepper to taste
    Garnish: Black Greek olives

Cut tomatoes into thin wedges. Peel and thin slice onion and cucumber. Thin slice the pepper. Chop purslane in large chunks. Toss veggies with other ingredients. Garnish each plate with several black olives.

PICNIC TURKEY SALAD

When turkeys first appeared in Europe, after Spanish ships brought them from the New World, a rumor started that they were large chickens from the Turkish Ottoman Empire. If you don't have meaty Roma tomatoes, use another variety but do remove seeds and juice.

    Salad:
1 lemon or other cucumber
3 TB olive oil
1 cup sliced mushrooms
1/4 cup chopped onion
2 cups cubed turkey (or chicken)
4 Roma tomatoes, chopped
    Dressing:
1/2 cup buttermilk or plain yogurt
1 TB cider vinegar
1 tsp spicy mustard
Salt and pepper to taste

Peel, seed and chop cucumber. Sauté mushrooms and onion. Cool, transfer to a bowl. Add turkey, tomatoes and cucumber. Mix dressing, stir it in. Chill one hour.

AUGUST TOMATO SALAD

Look for heirlooms, delectable old varieties grown only for flavor and at their peak of perfection in late August.

6 perfect summer tomatoes
1/4 cup minced fresh herbs
1/3 cup olive oil
3 TB cider vinegar
Salt and pepper to taste

Cut tomatoes into wedges and remove seedy centers. Toss the rest with the other ingredients and serve at once, before the tomatoes begin to go soft.

Fall Salads

FALL GREENS AND APPLES   A French farm salad

1 cup walnut meats
1/4 cup olive oil
2 TB fresh rosemary leaves
4 cups greens
2 crisp apples, cored and sliced thin
Balsmic vinaigrette dressing

Sauté nuts and rosemary in oil until nuts begin to brown. Spread lettuce and other greens on individual plates. Arrange thin sliced apples beside the greens. Top with rosemary-walnuts and an oil and vinegar dressing. Add a succulent crumbled bleu cheese and warm cornbread and call it lunch.

APPLE AND LEEK SALAD

This tangy fall combination is popular in Poland, where it's called Pikantna Salatka z Jablek i Porow. No kidding.

2 tart apples, cored, peeled and chopped
2 leeks, white plus soft green parts, chopped
2 TB cider vinegar
4 TB canola oil
Salt and pepper to taste
Lettuce or watercress

Prepare apples and leeks, then toss and mix them. Mix vinegar, oil and salt and pour over the salad. On individual salad plates, arrange beds of lettuce or watercress, then place a scoop of the salad on top of each.

FALL MUSHROOM MARINADE

1 pound any fresh mushrooms
1/2 cup olive oil
1/4 cup aged vinegar
2 TB minced fresh herbs
Salt and pepper to taste

Brush dry mushrooms to clean them, then slice them thin. Toss with other ingredients, then refrigerate in a covered container 6 to 24 hours before eating. Keeps about 5 days.

FALL PEARS AND CHICKEN

    Salad:
Lettuce or greens to line the plates
1 pound cooked chicken breast
3 large firm pears
    Dressing:
1/3 cup wine vinegar
3 TB olive oil
1 tsp crumbled dry tarragon
1 tsp warm honey
Salt and pepper to taste
    Garnish: Chopped fresh mint leaves

Mix the dressing ingredients first and set aside. Line four salad plates with lettuce. Slice the chicken and arrange it on the lettuce.

Once cut, pears quickly brown. So wait until just before serving, then peel and slice the pears and arrange them beside the chicken.

Keep pears and apples from browning by sprinkling them with lemon juice, or with ascorbic acid powder, also known as sour salt or vitamin C powder. Drizzle dressing over the salads. Garnish with fresh mint.

OCTOBER SLAW

    Salad:
1 cup cabbage, sliced thin
1/2 red onion, thin sliced
1 carrot, grated
1 tart apple -- core and grate
3 TB minced mint
1/2 cup raisins
    Dressing:
1/4 cup warm honey
1/4 cup plain yogurt or buttermilk
1 TB cider vinegar
Salt and pepper to taste

Cut cabbage in quarters, then remove the outer leaves and core. Thin slice. Prepare other ingredients, mix the dressing and toss all together. Optional additions include chopped dandelion greens, chopped watercress, grated kohlrabi.

CHICKEN SALAD WITH ARUGULA

Arugula is incredibly easy to grow here. Plant it in March, and again in August for a crop that will keep you in green salads until after Christmas.

2 packed cups arugula
1/2 cup balsamic vinaigrette dressing
2 cups fresh or thawed frozen berries
1 pound cooked chicken breasts, sliced thin
1 cup crumbled bleu cheese
1/4 cup chopped green onion
8 slices artisan bread, toasted and buttered.

Toss leaves with dressing. Divide into four bowls. Arrange berries, then chicken slices. Crumble on bleu cheese and scatter green onion. Serve with two slices of warm buttered toast tucked into the side of each salad.

APPLE BEET SALAD

If you like beets, you'll love them with apples and walnuts.

    Salad:
2 large beets – simmer until soft
Leaves of the two beets, cleaned
1 large carrot, grated
2 tart crisp apples, chopped
1 cup walnuts, chopped
1/2 cup flat leaf Italian parsley

Dressing:
3 TB apple cider
3 TB cider vinegar
1/3 cup canola oil
1 TB Dijon mustard
2 cloves garlic, smashed and minced

Peel and slice cooked beets, add grated carrot, chopped apple, nuts and chopped beet leaves. Save beet stems for the stockpot. Combine dressing ingredients and toss with the vegetables.

ROASTED BEET SALAD

Roast extra beets as long as you're roasting, since this brings out their best flavor. Use them later as a side dish, or in soup. Roasting gives this salad its unique appeal.

2 medium beets
2 packed cups arugula
1 cup mixed greens
4 oz crumbled bleu or gorgonzola cheese
1/2 cup toasted chopped filberts
 Vinaigrette dressing

Wash, peel and oil beets, then wrap each one in foil to keep moisture in. Roast them at 425F 50 minutes or until a fork goes in easily. Unwrap, cool and slice them. Lay out greens on four salad plates, then sliced beets on top of them. Crumble on the cheese and scatter the roasted nuts. Serve with a vinaigrette dressing.

BERRY BEET SALAD

Just about any frozen berries will do. I like to pick plenty or wild blackberries in August and tuck them in the freezer.

2 medium beets
1 cup frozen berries
3 TB red wine vinegar
3 TB olive oil
1/2 tsp dill weed
Salt to taste
2 cups mixed greens

Wash, trim and cut beets into quarters. Don't peel yet. Simmer them about 20 minutes or until a fork goes in. Cool and rub off skin, then slice thin. Partially thaw berries and toss them with beets, oil, vinegar, dill and salt. Serve on a bed of greens. For variety, lay slices of apple or pear on each salad plate. Don't toss them with the beets or they will turn splotchy red.

Salads for Winter

In the old days, pickled fruits and vegetables, spicy kim chi and tart sauerkraut in winter provided the acidic rush and vitamin-rich crunch that our bodies need. Frozen foods pack a similar punch, but canned foods, heated to high temperatures, lack vitamin C and other nutrients we obtain from fresh foods. We may afford long-distance transport and refrigerated shipping that deliver any food, from any climate, at any time. Yet some of the old favorites and local crops are better for our health and certainly represent wiser resource use.

FRENCH FRUIT PLATE

This salad is elegant in its simplicity, like so much of the food we've learned about from the French.

2 winter pears
1 cup roasted walnuts
1/2 pound chunk of Gorgonzola or bleu cheese

Cut pears in wedges, remove core and lay them on a platter with a small bowl of walnuts and chunk of cheese with a spreading knife. Serve with wheat crackers or small toasts.

JOE'S CARROT SALAD

As with all our family recipes, this one can be endlessly varied around the central theme. When the berries are ripe, they make a fine addition, or use thawed berries, frozen last summer.

    Salad:
3 large carrots coarsely grated
1/3 cup fresh and/or dry fruit
1/3 cup total of roasted nuts or seeds
    Dressing:
1/4 cup lemon juice
1/4 cup mild oil
2 or 3 TB warm honey
1/2 tsp salt.

Toss all together and serve it cold.

ROMAINE SALAD WITH DRIED FRUIT

Serve this when most of the salad makings of summer are unavailable. I love dates in this salad but any dry fruit provides texture, flavor and vitamins.

One head of Romaine lettuce
1/3 cup chopped dry fruit
1/2 cup chopped walnuts
1/3 cup balsamic vinaigrette dressing
1 tsp sugar
1/4 cup soft goat cheese

Clean and separate leaves and put five or six for each person in a large bowl. Stir sugar into the dressing. Toss leaves with dressing until you coat each large leaf. Divide onto salad plates and add dates, nuts and goat cheese to each.

WINTER BROCCOLI SALAD

1 cup broccoli chunks
1 cup thin sliced carrots
1/4 cup each: sliced dill pickle, thin sliced onion
1/2 cup chopped nuts

Lightly steam chunks of broccoli and sliced carrots until al dente, barely cooked. Dunk them in cold water to stop the cooking, then chill them. Toss with other ingredients and an oil and vinegar dressing.

WINTER GREEN SALAD

Instead of kohlrabi, you can use a beet, or a couple of carrots lightly cooked, to add color and body to this healthful salad of dark-season greens, and berries frozen in August. Good greens include arugula, watercress, dandelion, beet tops, chard, calendula etc.

3 cups available salad greens
1 cup kohlrabi, peeled and diced
1/2 cup walnut meats or sunflower seeds
1/2 cup thawed frozen berries, or one grated apple
Balsamic vinaigrette
    Garnish: Crumbled feta cheese

In a covered bowl with a little water, microwave kohlrabi two minutes. Cool it. Prepare other ingredients then add kohlrabi pieces. Dress with a balsamic vinaigrette. Sprinkle with crumbled feta.

FENNEL AND WATERCRESS

1/2 cup dried cranberries
1/3 cup balsamic vinaigrette dressing
1 large bunch of watercress (or arugula)
2 fennel bulbs, thin sliced
1/2 cup chopped filberts

Soak cranberries in dressing for a few minutes, to soften, while you clean the watercress. Use the leaves only. Stems can be cut up and used in soups. In a bowl, toss watercress and fennel with oil and vinegar dressing and cranberries. Add nuts and toss again.

BEET AND FENNEL SALAD

1 beet
1 cup tender beet greens
1 tart apple -- core and chop
1 fennel bulb, thin sliced
1 cup shredded cabbage
2 tsp dry dill weed
Oil and vinegar dressing

Cook the whole clean beet in water until it is soft. Cool, peel and slice. Prepare other fresh vegetables and toss it all with the dill and dressing. A tasty accompaniment is toast spread with goat cheese.

APPLE SLAW

    Salad:
2 tart apples, cored and cut into matchsticks
2 stalks celery, chopped
1/4 cup minced fresh parsley
1/4 cup toasted sunflower seeds
    Dressing:
1/4 cup plain yogurt
1 TB canola oil
Salt and pepper to taste

Since tart apples quickly turn brown in the air, get them into the dressing as fast as you can. Toss all ingredients together in a big mixing bowl, then transfer to a pretty serving bowl.

GOURMET BEET SALAD

The beets bake a long time, so start this one early. Other than the long bake, it's simple.
Oven at 350F

3 medium beets
1/2 cup walnuts
1 TB olive oil
1 tsp fresh rosemary, minced
1/4 cup minced onion
1/2 tsp sugar
1/2 cup vinaigrette dressing
2 cups young greens
    Garnish: 2 ounces fresh goat cheese

Wrap each beet in foil and place them in a baking dish. Bake 90 minutes. In a fry pan, sauté walnuts and rosemary in the oil until nuts begin to brown. Set them aside to cool. When beets are done, unwrap and cool them under cold water while rubbing off the skins.

Cut beets into wedges and toss with nuts and rosemary, onion, sugar and vinaigrette. Divide greens on four plates then top with the beet mix. Crumble goat cheese over each.

WINTER KOHLRABI SALAD

Kohlrabi is incredibly easy to grow in our climate, a neglected but mild and delicious vegetable with a rich nutty flavor, good both raw and cooked. Plant in late summer for a crop you can harvest most of the winter.

Salad:
1 medium kohlrabi bulb
1 carrot grated
1/2 cup wild dandelion or other dark greens
Dressing:
1 TB white vinegar
2 TB soy sauce
1 TB sesame oil
1 TB canola oil
1 tsp honey

Peel and thin slice the kohlrabi. Grate the carrot and chop the greens. Put them in a bowl and dress them an hour in advance of eating so flavor soaks in. Another version of this salad can be made using chopped kohlrabi, steamed about two minutes, so it's partially cooked.

FERMENTED RADDISH SALAD

Whey seeps out of yogurt, and is what remains during cheese making after the milk solids are removed. Yogurt whey is a good source of micro-organisms that ferment vegetables, thus adding important nutrients. Fermentation creates acidity so preserves vegetables without refrigeration.

10 to 12 large red radishes, sliced thin
2 cloves garlic, minced
3 TB soy sauce
1 TB white vinegar
1 tsp sugar
2 tsp sesame oil
2 TB yogurt whey

Instead of radishes, you can also use one large daikon. Gently crush sliced radishes with a large spoon, so they keep their shape but liquids can penetrate. Place them in a sterile jar and pour over them a mix of the other ingredients. Screw on a tight, sterile lid and let them sit at room temperature for 24 hours so the whey can begin the vitamin-enriching fermentation. Eat now or save in the refrigerator up to several months.

Making Salad Dressings

The word salad derives from the Latin *salata*, salted. The ancients treasured tender herbs and greens but knew they needed dressing to be at their best. Olive oil and something sour like wine that had turned to vinegar, plus a good sprinkle of salt served our Mediterranean ancestors.

Today, commercial salad dressings are expensive and contain chemicals to tingle your taste buds, or to preserve the product on a shelf for a year. It looks to me like an industry largely built on our not knowing how many great dressings are simple and quick to make from a few common ingredients.

ABOUT COOKING OILS

The full story on oils and fats and our health is complex, and it's not the story most of us have read in the popular press. But here are some basics. The best oils are cold pressed, at below 120 degrees F, and provide the most "good" Omega 3 fats. Expeller pressed oils have been exposed to heat, up to 300F, and may include solvents to preserve them. A generic vegetable oil is a mix of different types, such as soy, corn and canola. Nearly all of the soy, corn and canola products available, not specified organic, come from Genetically Modified Organisms (GMO).

Special oils such as sesame, walnut, grape seed, etc. are sold in small quantities and used as special flavorings. Less refining in any oil means that more natural micro-nutrients remain, but unrefined oils are damaged by heat over 225F, so don't use them for frying. Coconut oil and safflower oil have high "smoke points" so are good bets for healthy frying. Avoid all hydrogenated fats. Store oils in a cool dark place. If the label suggests refrigerating, do that. Olive oil keeps a very long time and is quite resistant to chemical changes. Any oil can be frozen without harm.

BALSAMIC VINAIGRETTE

People who know food insist that excellent balsamic vinegar is absolutely worth it. It only takes a little bit, so indulge. The Epicenter website recommends two very good, reasonably priced balsamic vinegars -- Caroliva Reserve and Masserie di Sant'Eramo. If you have to fake it, add a little sugar or honey to your average vinegar.

4 TB aged balsamic vinegar
1 tsp prepared Dijon mustard
1 clove garlic
3/4 cup extra virgin olive oil
Salt and fresh ground pepper to taste

Squeeze garlic through a garlic press. In a blender, puree all ingredients. Store in a screw-top bottle, in the refrigerator (fresh garlic can spoil) and mix well before each use. One cup dresses 8 servings. Try substituting some walnut oil for olive, to make walnut vinaigrette. For herbal vinaigrette, add one teaspoon of tarragon and one of rosemary, before the puree step.

OIL AND VINEGAR DRESSING

1 cup extra virgin olive oil
1/3 cup cider vinegar or red wine vinegar
2 TB dark soy sauce or 2 tsp salt
1 tsp dry mustard or prepared Dijon
1 tsp sugar or 1/2 tsp honey

Sugar or honey can bring welcome sweetness to a salad that balsamic vinegars provide with more subtle flavors. Shake the dressing well before serving. Store in a tight-lidded bottle such as an old-style German beer bottle, or a recycled, relabeled plastic squeeze bottle. Keeps for weeks. Needs no refrigeration.

CREAMY VINAIGRETTE

1/3 cup red wine vinegar
2/3 cup heavy cream or crème fraiche
1 tsp salt
1/4 tsp pepper
1 Tb fresh herbs

Wisk all together then set aside at least 20 minutes, so flavors can meld. Store in the refrigerator.

ITALIAN DRESSING

1/2 cup red wine vinegar
1 tsp each: salt, fresh ground black pepper, sugar,
    garlic powder
1 TB dry parsley flakes
1/4 cup grated Parmesan
1-1/2 cup olive oil

Shake all ingredients in a tightly closed glass jar. Because it contains no fresh ingredients, the dressing will keep several weeks at room temperature.

HONEY LEMON GARLIC DRESSING

4 cloves garlic, crushed and minced
1/2 cup olive oil
1/2 cup fresh lemon juice
2 TB warm honey
Salt and pepper to taste

Sauté garlic in oil, then whisk in other ingredients. Keeps in the refrigerator up to two weeks.

STRAWBERRY VINAIGRETTE

From May into early July local strawberries are ripe and luscious. If you grow an "ever bearing" variety, you'll have a few until the first frost. For the best in farm berries, visit a u-pick farm, in clothes you don't mind getting stained. Makes almost three cups of delicious salad dressing.

1 cup very ripe smashed berries
8 cloves garlic, chopped
1/2 medium onion, chopped
1 TB each: Dijon mustard, minced parsley, soy sauce
1/4 cup lemon juice
1/4 cup cider vinegar
1 cup canola oil
Salt and pepper to taste

Puree all together. Store in a tightly covered glass jar and shake before using.

BUTTERMILK DRESSING

1 cup buttermilk
1 tsp garlic powder or 2 cloves smashed and minced
1 tsp salt
Pepper to taste

Mix well. Chilled, it keeps up to two weeks.

SAVORY YOGURT DRESSING

1 cup plain yogurt
1/2 cup olive oil
1 tsp each: dry chives, dry parsley, dry dill weed, garlic powder
Salt and pepper to taste

Mix well. Store chilled. Shake before using

EGG DISHES

Eggs taste fairly similar whether from chickens, ducks, quail or turkeys. Or so I am told. I've only tried chicken eggs, but I've eaten them from Albany to Zurich. The main difference seems to be whether the bird ran free and ate bugs, or grew up in a little cage, eating commercial feed. Dark, sturdy, flavorful yolks result from a wild and complex diet that hens obtain by pecking around outdoors.

Few of our eggs have such simple origins, but people I know who keep two or three hens in town swear by them as fabulous insect eaters in the yard, and suppliers of nearly effortless, high quality and very tasty protein.

We kept a dozen hens when we lived in Central Oregon. It was simple and satisfying, but we've not taken the time to construct a henhouse where we live now. We get our eggs from a farm west of Junction City, where a friend's parents live and work.

Commercial organic, free-range eggs mean chickens live a more normal life, if "organic" flocks of thousands, with one little door to permit outdoor activity, can be imagined as normal. At least they get more space, better food and no hormones or antibiotics.

Boiling Eggs

PERFECT HARD BOILED EGGS

A perfect egg will be easy to peel and have no greenish color on the yolk, caused by cooking too long. Eggs less that a week old will be hard to peel no matter how you hard-boil them. Start eggs in cold or tepid water, or they may crack as the air inside suddenly expands. Cover them with water an inch above their tops.
Start timing when the first bubbles begin to rise. A soft boiled large egg with runny yolk and firm white takes about 4-1/2 minutes. A hard boil with a solid yolk takes at least ten minutes. If you boil an egg too long you'll find a greenish coating around the yolk. As soon as the time is up, dunk eggs in cold running water to stop the cooking and to loosen the shells and help them peel easily. Using an alternate method, as soon as the pan achieves a good rolling boil, take it off the heat and start timing then.

SIMPLE DEVILED EGGS

Prepare eggs as above. When they are cool, slice each one in two, the LONG way. Gently remove yolks into a bowl. Add mayonnaise, a little vinegar, prepared mustard, salt and pepper and mix these into the yolks to form a paste. Refill the whites with the paste preparation. Sprinkle parsley or paprika on top, or for a bit of a bite use chipotle chili powder.

CURRIED DEVILED EGGS

8 eggs, boiled 10 minutes
1/4 cup mayonnaise
2 TB olive oil
2 tsp lemon juice
1 TB curry powder
1/4 cup minced walnuts
1/2 tsp each: salt, pepper
    Garnish: A sprinkle of paprika

Quickly cool eggs in cold water. Crack the shells and slip them off. Add shells to your compost to give back some calcium. Cut eggs in half the long way, remove yolks and mix them with the other ingredients, then use the mix to refill the eggs. Serve cold, garnished with a sprinkle of red paprika.

CAULIFLOWER PUREE WITH EGGS

This dish was served at a glorious society wedding in Tuscany, one of a dozen dishes, featured in a lovely magazine called *Cucina Italiana*, and the only one I thought I could make at home. The eggs are poached in a vegetable puree. It was originally made with two quail eggs per diner.

5 cups chopped cauliflower
1 large carrot, peeled, cut in thirds
1 cup water
1 TB olive oil
1/2 tsp salt
4 eggs
1 tsp white vinegar
Pepper to taste
2 cups water
    Garnish: Warm pita or sour dough bread

Simmer together 20 minutes: cauliflower, carrot, water, oil, salt. Remove carrot. It was just for flavoring. Puree the cauliflower with 1/2 cup of the cooking liquid, then add the rest of the liquid and puree it again. Return it to the pot to stay warm.

Boil two cups of water, add the vinegar and then crack four eggs and drop them in. Poach until the whites are set. Divide the puree into four pretty bowls. Drop one poached egg into the center of each bowl of puree. Serve in bowls on plates, each accompanied by two quarters of warm pita or thin sliced sour dough bread.

Fried Egg Dishes

HUNGARIAN OMELET

1 small onion, thin sliced
4 TB butter
2 green peppers, diced
2 firm tomatoes, diced
Salt and pepper to taste
5 beaten eggs

Sauté onion in butter until soft, then add peppers and cook over low heat ten minutes. Add tomatoes, salt and pepper and simmer five minutes. Add eggs and stir until they are set. Serve hot. Good with sourdough bread.

SINGAPORE EGG FRIED RICE

Tropical Singapore has an amazing variety of "hawkers" and food stalls specializing in unique local dishes, where seating is outdoors. (Thanks to Beng See Lim for taking us to her favorites.) Try substituting one cup of edible pod peas or frozen peas for the chopped green beans.

3 cups cooked rice
1 cup diced chicken
1/4 cup olive oil
1 tsp ginger powder
Salt and pepper to taste
1 medium onion, chopped
1 cup chopped green beans
3 beaten eggs
2 TB soy sauce
2 TB curry powder

Cook one and a half cups rice in three cups water. A stir-fry is hot and fast, very energy-efficient. Have hot rice in a serving bowl before you start the stir-fry. Meanwhile, sauté cooked chicken in oil with ginger, salt and pepper, onion and green beans. Add beaten eggs. Cook over high heat for one minute, while stirring. Move this hot mixture to a platter. Serve over rice.

FRITATTAS

Big, well-seasoned egg fritters, popular in Italy, are a good way to use vegetables and cheese. Some cooks flip them over to cook the second side, a tricky move. I prefer to finish the frittata under a hot broiler. In the dark seasons, substitute thin-sliced cooked white or red potatoes for the zucchinis. For a Greek slant, use feta cheese and add come chopped Greek olives. And soaked sun- dried tomatoes, if you like.

1/2 onion, thin sliced
3 cloves garlic, minced
2 zucchinis, thin sliced
1/4 cup minced parsley
1/2 tsp each: dry rosemary, thyme and sage
Salt and pepper to taste
1/4 cup olive oil
6 to 10 large eggs, beaten
1/2 cup chopped ham or chicken (optional)
1/2 cup fresh grated cheese

In an oven-proof fry pan, sauté all the veggies, and garlic in half the oil until tender, then add salt and pepper. Transfer hot veggies to a mixing bowl, cool a bit, then mix in the eggs. Wipe out the fry pan so no veggies remain, or they will burn. Add more oil and heat the pan again.

Pour in the egg and veggie mixture and tilt the pan so it spreads to cover the bottom. Sprinkle in meat and cheese. Cook until the bottom is light brown.

Place the pan about 8 inches below the oven's broiler element and cook three to six minutes, with the oven open so you can watch. Remove it when the top just starts to brown. Serve warm with tomato slices and hearty bread or toast.

Baking your Eggs

SIMPLE BAKED EGGS

Shirred eggs or oeufs en cocotte are an easy treat, with many tasty variations. Each egg will have it's own little dish or ramekin. Start with one tablespoon of melted butter and another of cream, in the bottom. Break a fresh egg on top of this.

Add a sprinkle of salt and pepper, then another tablespoon of cream on top. Set the little dishes in a pan with an inch of water. Cover them with foil or a lid to keep steam in.

Place the pan in a 350F oven, or leave atop the stove on a low burner. Simmer 12 minutes for a soft boil, 15 for medium, 20 for hard. Most variants call for additions that go in before the egg. Try a tablespoon of chorizo sausage, or smoked fish, or a tablespoon of mixed fresh herbs in Dijon mustard. A nice finish is a bit of grated hard cheese on top.

QUICHE DE JOUR

Quiche keeps several days in the refrigerator. Contrary to urban legend, real men do eat it -- in any of its dozens of incarnations. Oven at 350F

1 uncooked piecrust or a layer of filo dough
2 cups milk or half-and-half
2 beaten eggs
1/2 tsp salt
1/2 tsp nutmeg
1 cup grated cheese
1 cup add-ons (see below)

Mix a filling of milk, eggs, salt and nutmeg. Pour this into the pie shell. Add grated cheese, any from cheddar to gruyere, and mix in. Now, select items to add...smoked salmon, leftover turkey or cooked vegetables, chopped onions, chopped garden greens. Salmon and sorrel makes a tasty combination. I usually make two or three at once. Each quiche can be different. The classic includes cooked bacon. Bake 60 to 80 minutes, or until filling sets and crust begins to brown.

RED WINE AND ONION QUICHE
Oven at 350F

1 unbaked pie shell
2 TB olive oil
3 cloves garlic, minced
1 small onion, diced
1 tsp each: oregano, thyme, basil
Salt and pepper to taste
1/2 cup red wine
1-1/2 cups milk
3 eggs, beaten
1 cup grated cheese (Edam is ideal)

Sauté garlic, onion, herbs, salt and pepper in oil until onions are soft. Whisk wine, milk and eggs together and pour into the unbaked pie shell. Add the onion mix and stir it in. Top with grated cheese. Bake one hour or until the filling is set.

LEEK TART

Make a piecrust, fill it with leeks, cheese, cream and eggs and you have a memorable centerpiece for a good meal, similar to a quiche. A delicious variant contains bacon and Gruyere cheese. Oven at 400F

Pastry:
1-1/2 cups flour
1/4 cup olive oil
1/4 cup melted butter
1/2 tsp salt
3 TB water
Filling:
12 leeks, cut into thin discs
1 beaten egg
1/2 cup cream
1/2 cup grated mild cheese
1 TB minced fresh parsley
1 TB minced fresh sage
1/2 tsp salt

Simmer leeks ten minutes in salted water to soften them. Mix pastry ingredients and form into a ball. Add water if needed, more flour if too wet. Press dough into a pie tin. Drain the leeks and add egg, cream, cheese, parsley, sage and salt. Mix well then pour this into the pie shell. Bake 25 to 35 minutes, or until liquids set.

HOLIDAY ONIONS

This dish is similar to the filling for leek tart, but has no crust. Oven at 375F

1 large white onion
1 tsp olive oil
1 TB butter
1 clove garlic, minced
Salt and pepper to taste
1 egg, beaten
1/2 cup milk
2 TB flour
3 ounces cheddar cheese, grated
1 tsp fresh sage, minced

Peel and cut onions into chunks, then sauté them in oil until they soften. Add butter and garlic, salt and pepper and cook 5 minutes more. Set aside. In a bowl, mix egg, milk and flour, then stir in cheese. Oil a casserole and put onions in it, then pour egg and cheese mixture over them. Stir gently. Bake 25 to 30 minutes. Serve hot with fresh sage sprinkled on top

LEEK AND SALMON CUSTARD

Custards can be much more than dessert food. This savory variant presents novel possibilities. Use cold-smoked salmon (never over 85F during smoking). It has a flexible but firm texture, like lox. This tasty dish is simple to create, with an impressive appearance. Oven at 350F

4 large leeks
1/4 tsp salt
8 ounces cold-smoked salmon
1 cup half-and-half
2 beaten eggs
1 tsp Dijon mustard
1/2 cup grated Gruyere cheese

Clean and trim the leeks then, in salted water in a fry pan, simmer the whole leeks until they are soft, about ten minutes. Drain and cool them. Divide the salmon and cut it into inch wide strips.

Wrap each leak with a spiral strip. Lay them in a buttered baking pan. Beat together the half-and-half, eggs, mustard and grated cheese. Pour this over the leeks and salmon. Bake 30 minutes until the custard is firm. Serve hot, one wrapped leek per person, with surrounding custard.

SAVORY BREAD PUDDING

Like custard, bread pudding is not just a sweet dish, and not just for dessert or breakfast. The original version of this recipe called for thin sliced asparagus, barely cooked but the dish is good with almost any combination of seasonal fresh vegetables. Serve it for lunch or a light supper. Oven at 350F

3 beaten eggs
2 cups milk
2 cups thin sliced, lightly cooked vegetables
2 TB fresh minced herbs
Salt and pepper to taste
6 slices sourdough bread, generously buttered
2 cups grated cheese

If the bread crust is chewy, remove it before buttering. Mix eggs, milk, vegetables, herbs, salt and pepper and pour a first layer into a casserole pan, about 1/2 inch thick.

Arrange slices of bread on top of this, then a layer of cheese. Repeat layers, until you use all the ingredients. Top with grated cheese. Place the casserole pan in a baking pan half full of water, in the oven. Bake 45 minutes or until the top begins to brown.

SWEDISH RUTABAGA PUDDING

This savory vegetable puree with milk and eggs makes a tasty fall or winter lunch. Oven at 350F

3 medium rutabagas
1/2 cup breadcrumbs
1/2 cup milk
2 beaten eggs
1/4 tsp nutmeg
2 TB butter
Salt and pepper to taste
1/2 cup grated cheese

Quarter, then simmer rutabagas about 20 minutes or until soft. Peel them and puree with other ingredients. Oil an 8x8 inch baking pan and pour in mixture. Stir in grated cheese. Bake one hour or until firm.

SAVORY PUMPKIN POTATO CUSTARD

Here's a lunch of savory flavors, made with pumpkin or any winter squash, eggs and cheese. Red or Yukon gold potatoes work best. Oven at 350F

2 cups cooked pumpkin
2 cups cooked potato chunks
1 onion, chopped
3 cloves garlic, minced
3 TB olive oil
1 tsp minced sage
1/4 tsp nutmeg
2 eggs, beaten
1 cup grated mild cheese

Puree together half the cooked pumpkin and potatoes. In a fry pan, sauté onion and garlic in the oil until onion is soft, then add sage and nutmeg and mix well. Remove from heat and add vegetable puree and eggs.
Spread remaining vegetable chunks in an oiled baking dish, then pour egg mix over them. Scatter grated cheese over the top. Bake one hour or until firm.

To the same hot pan, add the eggs and scramble them quickly with salt and pepper. Remove the pan from heat, and add back the cooked rice and the chicken and vegetable mixture. Re-warm while mixing everything together.

Making Crepes

Crepes are so popular in France that kids buy them from street stands on their way home from school. Filled with vegetables, or a meat or seafood mix, and rolled up, they make a meal. Filled with sugar, whipped cream or sweet fruit, they're dessert.

If you get into crepe making, you may want a real crepe pan. Otherwise, cook them on a ten-inch cast-iron or nonstick pan, or use a griddle. This recipe should make 12 crepes, depending on their size. Cook the crepes on medium high heat, then keep them warm until all are made and filled. In a café near us, they store them chilled and warm them in hot water just before serving.

CREPES

    Batter:
1 cup flour
1/2 tsp salt
3 large eggs, beaten
1 cup milk
1 cup water
2 TB minced fresh herbs (thyme, oregano, savory, chives, marjoram)
3 TB melted butter

Put the flour and salt in a large bowl. Slowly add eggs, milk and water, while stirring. Then stir in the herbs. Set the batter aside for at least an hour.
Just before frying the crepes, add melted butter to the batter for an unbeatably rich flavor.

Pour some batter then do a little rock and roll wrist action to spread the batter so it's thin. Cook until the bottom is light brown and the top is full of bubbles. Flip over and cook briefly. Slide out onto a plate or pie tin, to keep warm in the oven.

SPINACH AND MUSHROOM CREPES

Thanks to Esther Caballero-Manrique for testing and improving this recipe.

Batter: see above

Filling:
5 cups chopped fresh spinach
1 cup sliced fresh mushrooms
2 cloves garlic, minced
4 TB butter
4 TB flour
1/2 cup milk or cream
2 TB soy sauce
1/2 tsp pepper
Garnish: 1 cup or more grated cheese

Sauté the spinach, mushrooms and garlic in the butter until mushrooms are tender. Sprinkle in the flour. Slowly add milk or cream as it thickens. Flavor with soy sauce and pepper. Put a few tablespoons of filling along the center of each crepe and roll it up.

Lay rolled crepes in a baking pan, side-by-side, and top with grated cheese. Place briefly under the broiler and watch it carefully, every moment while the cheese melts.

SEAFOOD

Our region produces plenty of wild caught salmon, halibut, farmed oysters and small pink shrimp, and dozens of other species. At the coast, clam digging and collecting plentiful mussels is a fun project. If you fish, you know what you like and where to catch it.

Outdoor Seafood

UNCLE CHARLIE'S BEACH SALMON

Lopez Island, August 1960: Charlie builds a bonfire of driftwood, about sunset. He pulls two large slabs of salmon filet out of his rubber fisherman's bag and arranges each in its own flat cage made of chicken wire. Mounted on driftwood poles in the sand, he stands one cage on each side of the fire.

Gulls call over the still sea. Friends appear on the trail carrying food. The fire burns down to shimmering coals. Atop the Olympic Range across the strait, snowfields reflect the last rosy sunshine. Charlie fusses with the arrangement, brushes melted butter on the fish, then settles back again, leaning on a log. About the time the stars come out, the whole crowd is feasting on the best fish in the world.

CEVICHE AT THE BEACH

El Salvador, 1972: Our host takes us to La Libertad, a tropical seaside town with offshore stacks that remind us of the Oregon Coast. We enjoy cold beers in a breezy restaurant above the surf. Our host orders a big platter. Qué es esto? Ceviche -raw fish. Is he kidding?

He explains that it's not technically raw, just uncooked. The strong acid marinade not only kills bacteria and parasites, but starts the pickling and breakdown of proteins, to be continued by stomach acids. We order another round of beers and dig in. It's love at first bite.

Turns out that uncooked fish provides a number of essential nutrients, which may be why those who enjoy it develop a craving. White fish are traditional, but I've had ceviche and its Japanese brother, sashimi, with a wide variety of fish and shellfish, including giant clam in Palau. Lobster, crab, shrimp, fresh water fish and red tuna are all good transformed in ceviche.

1/2 pound firm fish
1/2 cup lemon or lime juice
1/2 onion thin sliced
Cayenne or fresh hot peppers, to taste
Optional:Chopped tomatoes, avocado, celery, cilantro

Use very fresh fish, clean and without bones. Ahi or yellowtail tuna are great, as are halibut or other firm fish. Cut fish into thin slices or bite-sized chunks. Marinade in a small bowl so that the fish is mostly covered with acidic juice. Let it "cook" at room temperature for at least an hour, then keep it cold. Ceviche will keep two or three days in the refrigerator. In some regions the fish is ground up first, but that's far from my favorite.

For Mexican and Central American ceviche (also spelled Sebiche), add lots of chopped fresh cilantro. This is my personal favorite. In Cuba, they add a sprinkling of allspice. South Americans like it with chopped tomatoes, celery or avocado in the marinade with the fish. Peruvians say ceviche was first made by the ancient, coastal Moche people. Latinos often enjoy it with something crunchy – popcorn, roasted corn, crackers or chips.

STEELHEAD ON THE CAMPFIRE

Santiam Pass, summer of 1980: My son and his pal Jason are wading in the lake when they catch a steelhead hung up on a snag and about 20 inches long. They bring it to me, still wiggling. We build a fire and fry it, sharing the treat flavored with nothing but a little salt. I'd forgotten how wonderful truly fresh fish could taste. Second best fish in the world.

GATHERING MUSSELS AT THE COAST

Bob Creek Wayside, spring 2012: Out on the rocks at low tide, we find mussels everywhere. We cut through the tough bissel fibers that glue mussels to the rocks, picking only the largest from the immense colonies that carpet the area. The surf is roaring and the wind is light. Back at the beach with loaded sacks, we fill buckets with salt water and drop in the mussels. Our harvest will ride home like this and a few days later, fed on some cornmeal, the green stuff will be gone from their guts and we'll have a family feast.

If you gather your own, watch that incoming tide. And observe posted signs. The season is closed when shellfish have fed on toxic marine plankton.

Scrape barnacles off mussel shells with the back of a knife and brush them clean under running water. Place live mussels in a bucket of salt water to which you've added half a cup of cornmeal. They will eat the meal and replace the bitter stuff that would otherwise fill their digestive organs.

Barely cook mussels or they will shrink and get tough. Quick steaming opens shells and leaves mussels tender. You can also broil, barbeque or bake them, or just toss them in the coals of a hot beach fire for about two minutes.

CAMPFIRE FISH FRY

Use fillets or chunks of fish. Heat the most heat-tolerant of fats -- olive oil, lard or beef fat to 350F. Make a quick and tasty dipping batter by mixing beer and flour, until texture is like heavy cream. Dip the fish in this and fry them in the fat. Serve with salt, and lemon juice or vinegar.

Stove Top Seafood

STEAMING OR POACHING FISH

In gentle heat, fish cook to a delicate flakiness. An easy way to steam fish is to start by placing fillets or a whole small fish on a heat-proof dish or plate.

Sprinkle lemon juice, oil, salt and pepper evenly. Add your chosen herbs then place the fish dish in an oversized fry pan. You want to keep the fish out of the water, but allow steam to cook the fish.

Add about 1/2 inch of water to the pan, keeping the fish dry. Cover tightly and steam for about five minutes. Or, leave out the plate and poach, as in the illustration. You can poach fish in well-seasoned water, but I prefer to steam the fish and keep more of the natural flavors. If you poach fish, save the water for stock.

STEAM FISH IN THE MICROWAVE

Despite the longtime prejudice of some gourmet cooks, the microwave oven is a fine poaching machine, according to French food scientist Herve' This. All wrong for meats, it's just right for nearly any fish, which will turn out tasty and succulent cooked at a temperature just below boiling.

1 to 1-1/2 pounds fish fillets
Juice of one half lemon
3 TB olive oil
Salt and pepper to taste

In a covered ovenproof glass or ceramic bowl, microwave cook fish until it's just flaky, two to four minutes. The time depends on volume and thickness, as well as on the wattage of the oven. Slice the second half of the lemon to serve with the fish.

FISH FILLETS IN PARCHMENT

Try this easy, tasty and impressive way to serve fish. A roll of parchment paper keeps forever and has many uses in the kitchen. Oven at 350F

1 to 2 pounds fish fillets
1 cup of a mix of celery, carrot and onion
2 TB fresh herbs
4 TB butter
4 TB white wine

Thin slice the vegetables. Blanche them in a large strainer by holding for one minute in boiling water, then drain.

Clean and remove all bones from fish. Set each the four servings of fish on a square of parchment paper. Atop each piece of fish, place 1/4 cup of the vegetables, 1TB butter, 1 TB wine and some of the herbs.

Roll paper to form a packet. Use beaten egg as glue if paper won't hold without help. Lay the packets on a baking dish or cookie sheet and cook until packets puff up, about ten minutes per inch of fish thickness.

SHELLFISH PASTA

20 to 30 big shiny black mussels
12 ounces dry linguini or other noodles
2 quarts, salted water
4 medium zucchini, sliced
2 medium tomatoes, chopped
1/4 cup chopped parsley
1/2 onion, chopped
1/2 cup olive oil

Boil the water over an open fire in large blackened pot. Add a few drops of oil and drop in the pasta. While water heats and pasta cooks, chop vegetables. Sauté them in oil, with salt and pepper. When they are cooked down, add the mussels, salt and pepper, cover the pan.

Simmer just two minutes then remove the pan from heat. Drain the pasta and keep it warm. Pick out any mussels that did not open and discard them. Serve pasta topped with sauce. Divide up the mussels, in their shells, to go atop the sauce.

SIMPLE SALMON SPREAD

Mix canned, smoked or cooked, fresh salmon with an equal or larger amount of warm, soft cream cheese. Add a little salt, thyme and parsley. Mix well with a fork. Serve on breakfast toast, with crackers or chips, or as a sandwich spread. It's excellent on thin sliced pumpernickel bread or tasty crackers.

SALMON TACOS

In Mexico, families pass bowls of tasty fillings around the table so each person can create tacos to taste. My cousin makes a taco bar buffet on a side table. Use soft warmed tortillas. Or fry them briefly in olive oil if you prefer. Examine the salmon fillets carefully and use pliers to pull out any pin-sized bones.

8 medium flour or 16 small corn tortillas
1 to 1-1/2 pound salmon fillet
Juice of one lime
Salt and pepper to taste

5 tomatoes, chopped
1 tsp each: chili powder, cumin
5 hot chilies, minced
1 large onion, sliced thin
1 to 2 cups sour cream
2 to 3 cups chopped lettuce or mixed greens

Season the salmon with lime juice, salt and pepper then grill or microwave poach it. Break it up into small pieces. Canned salmon will do.

Prepare separate bowls of other fillings. Season the chopped tomatoes with chili powder and cumin. Sprinkle tortillas with a few drops of water then warm them in the oven, wrapped in foil. When the makings are assembled, it's time to eat.

SALMON CAKES

Laurel Kincl tested and refined this recipe and declared it great for people who can't tolerate gluten. She suspected it would become part of her family repertoire of favorites. These cakes can be baked in the oven too, but won't have the nice, crisp outer crust that develops during frying.

3 cups cooked mashed potatoes
1 cup smoked or leftover cooked salmon
2 beaten eggs
1/2 cup chopped green onions
1 tsp each: dry sage, dry oregano
Salt and pepper to taste
Olive oil for frying
   Garnish: sour cream or a sauce of mayonnaise and pickle relish.

If you don't start out with a supply of precooked mashed potatoes, start by boiling the potatoes. While they cook break fish into pieces, beat eggs and chop green onion. Drain and mash the potatoes.

Mix them with other ingredients, except oil. Form into flat, round cakes. Fry cakes in oil, ideally in a well-seasoned cast iron pan, until light brown -- about three minutes on each side, medium heat. Serve hot, garnished with sour cream.

SALMON CHOWDER

The tastiest fish stock is made from bones and trimmings of a large salmon, simmered an hour in a large pot, and cooled. Don't use tails, fins or gills as they add bitterness. If you're ambitious, you can pick all the meat off the bones. Strain stock and discard bones and skin.

If you are not currently in possession of a fresh salmon carcass, ask your local fish merchant for "pet scraps." Give your cat and dog some of the wonderful cooled, calcium-rich broth. Then use the rest for soup. Of course, canned salmon will do, and this is a good way to use it.

1 pound cooked or one 15-ounce can salmon
4 TB butter (1/2 stick)
1 medium onion, chopped
3 cups diced potatoes
3 stalks celery, with tops, chopped
2 cloves garlic, minced
1 tsp thyme
3 TB flour

2 cups stock
2 cups whole milk
Salt and pepper to taste

Flake the salmon and set aside. In a fry pan, melt the butter then slowly cook the onion, potatoes, celery and garlic about seven minutes. Add thyme. Sprinkle the flour over everything then stir it in. Slowly add stock and milk as the soup thickens. Add salmon. Keep soup hot but do not boil. Add salt and pepper then serve hot. Try a pat of butter melted into each bowl.

CIOPPINO, SUMMER SEAFOOD STEW

Brought to the California coast by Italian and Portuguese fishermen, this hearty catch-all is a great meal with white wine and artisan breads. San Francisco chefs rarely include the greens. French Bouillabaisse (BOO ya baze) is similar to chioppin, (cho-PEEN-o) but includes herbs and spices - garlic, orange peel, basil, bay leaf, fennel and saffron.

2 pounds fish, and/or shellfish, shrimp, lobster, crab
4 large tomatoes
1 summer squash
1 medium onion
4 cloves garlic, minced
2 tsp thyme
2 cups packed spinach or other greens
1 quart water or fish stock
Salt and pepper to taste

Chop all the vegetables. Put vegetables, plus water or stock in a large pot. Add fish. Cover and simmer 20 minutes. Add shellfish to the pot five minute before the end, so they don't overcook and get tough. Serve hot.

VERACRUZ SHRIMP

Serve shrimp in a tasty sauce over cooked rice.

1 pound shrimp, peeled and de-veined
3 TB olive oil
1 medium onion
2 garlic cloves, minced
3 tomatoes
2 tsp chopped fresh jalapeno pepper
1 bell pepper
Salt to taste
1 TB cornstarch mixed with 2 TB water
2 cups hot cooked brown or white rice
    Garnish: 1/4 cup chopped cilantro, lime wedges.

Chop onion and tomatoes. Sauté the onion and garlic in olive oil, until soft. Add the tomatoes and jalapenos. Simmer 10 minutes, uncovered to reduce liquid.

Remove seeds and cut the green pepper into thin strips. To the pot, add these strips, salt and shrimp, then simmer 5 minutes. Add the cornstarch and water mix and stir until the sauce thickens, about 1 minute.

Divide the hot rice among four shallow soup bowls, then add the shrimp and vegetables to each bowl. Garnish with fresh cilantro and lime wedges.

MUSTARD GARNISHED SHRIMP

1 pound shrimp, shelled and de-veined
1/4 cup olive oil
1/2 teaspoon caraway or fennel seeds
Cayenne pepper to taste
4 cloves garlic, minced
2 TB Dijon mustard
1/4 cup lemon juice
2 TB Dijon mustard
Salt to taste
Serve over cooked rice

Start the white rice (one cup dry rice plus two cups water, with a dash of salt, simmered for 15 minutes) when you start preparing the shrimp and they should be ready at the same time. Brown rice takes 45 minutes.

In hot oil, sauté the caraway or fennel and cayenne pepper two minutes. Keep the vent fan on. Hot cayenne can irritate your nose or eyes. Add garlic and cook 3 minutes more. Add the shrimp, mustard, lemon juice and salt. Stir well. Cover the pan and simmer for five minutes. Serve this tasty mixture over rice, with a big salad and crusty bread.

CLAMS IN WHITE WINE

Prepare cooked pasta
   Sauce:
4 pounds fresh clams, in shells
1 cup water
8 cloves garlic, chopped
1/4 cup olive oil
1/4 cup white wine
3 TB minced fresh parsley

Heat salted water to boiling and drop in the pasta to cook until tender. See below for more on cleaning clams. Scrub the closed clamshells. Steam them over one cup of water. Remove them as they open and let them cool. Strain the water and set aside for the sauce.

Fry the garlic in the oil until it starts to soften, then add flour and mix to form a roux or paste. Add the wine and clam water slowly as the sauce thickens. Add cooked clams to this sauce. Drain cooked pasta. Serve sauce with clams over the pasta, sprinkled with minced fresh parsley.

Oven Baked Seafood

GARDEN VEGGIE BAKED STEELHEAD

Plain steelhead salmon, steamed, baked or broiled is incredibly tasty with a squeeze of lemon and sprinkling of salt. But when the garden's overflowing produce, I like to use it to enhance good fish. Oven at 350F

2 pounds steelhead or salmon fillets
2 cups chopped tomatoes
1 cup chopped mild peppers
1 medium onion, chopped
Salt and pepper to taste
1/2 cup walnuts
1/2 stick of butter (1/4 cup)

Soak nuts in melted butter (or in olive oil) 20 minutes. Mix chopped vegetables, salt and pepper and spread them in a large baking pan. Lay salmon on top of this bed. Cover the top of the fish with the buttery nuts. Bake about 25 to 40 minutes, depending on thickness of fish.

TROUT WITH SPINACH BUTTER

Fresh caught trout deserves special treatment and a wonderful rich sauce. Oven at 375F

4 small trout
4 TB butter
4 sprigs fresh fennel leaves
    Sauce:
1 stick butter
1/2 cup cream
1/2 cup cooked spinach, minced
Salt and pepper to taste

Clean the fish inside and out. Into the center of each put a tablespoon of butter, two sprigs of fennel, salt and pepper. Wrap each fish tightly in foil. Place them, well separated, on a cookie sheet. Bake 30 minutes. While they cook make the sauce. In a small saucepan, melt the butter then add the cream. Simmer over low heat about ten minutes to reduce the volume. Add minced spinach, salt and pepper, and mix well.

Remove fish from the oven after 30 minutes. Careful not to scald your hands, unwrap them. Pour the juice into the sauce. To serve, remove fish skin and divide fillets onto four plates. Spoon on sauce just before serving.

SHRIMP TART

Use filo dough or puff pastry for the shell if you don't want to make pie dough. The packaged dough freezes well. To clean fresh-caught shrimp, remove the heads to save for stock. With the underside up, tug on the fan-shaped tail and lift out the trail (dark "vein"), the intestine. Oven at 350F

1 unbaked pie shell
Shrimp to fill the shell
1/4 cup olive oil
1/2 cup minced fresh parsley
1 TB minced garlic
Salt and pepper to taste
1 cup stock
1 egg, beaten

In a bowl, toss cleaned shrimp with oil, parsley, garlic, salt and pepper. Leave them for 15 minutes, so the shrimp soaks up oil and flavors. Put all of this into the pie shell. Mix egg and stock, adding herbs and salt if you choose. Pour this over the shrimp.

Bake 40 minutes, or until the egg is set.

BAKED STUFFED MUSSELS

Use mussels that have fed on cornmeal, or remove greenish gut contents after cooking. Oven at 400F

20 to 30 mussels
1/2 cup water for steaming
2 TB olive oil
1/4 cup chopped onion
2 cloves garlic, minced
1 cup cooked or frozen spinach, chopped
1/2 cup dry bread crumbs
3 TB roasted sunflower seeds
3 TB golden raisins
1 tsp dry dill weed
1/4 tsp salt

In a large pot, steam mussels in the water until they open. Discard any that did not open. They were dead. Using a slotted spoon, lift shells from water and take out the meat, cutting the adductor muscle free so it's not wasted.

Chop the meat and set it aside. Separate and wash the shells so they are ready for filling. You will use fewer than half the shells you have. Strain cooking water and save it.

In a fry pan, sauté the onion and garlic in the olive oil about five minutes. Wrap the spinach in a cotton towel, squeeze it dry then add it to the fry pan, along with 2 TB of the saved cooking water. Cook about five minutes more. Remove the pan from heat. Add other ingredients and mix well.

Fill the clean mussel shells with this mixture. Shape the filling with your hands. Lay filled shells on a cookie sheet, cover with foil and bake about 7 minutes. Save the remaining cooking water for stock.

Making Fish Stock

The basis of great seafood soups, an excellent stock can be made by boiling filleted fish carcasses and heads from which gills are removed. Make a big batch when you have the resources, and freeze some for later.

In a soup kettle put 1/2 cup olive oil, 2 cups of chopped onions and/or leeks, 2 cups chopped fresh tomatoes, or 1/2 cup tomato paste in winter. Add 5 garlic cloves, 1 tsp each basil and dry orange peel, 1/2 tsp fennel or anis seeds, 2 pinches of saffron if you have it. Saute all these together about five minutes, or until onions are soft. Add fish trimmings, 2 quarts of water and 1 TB salt. Boil hard, skim off any scum, cover and simmer 45 minutes. Cool and strain through a large mesh sieve. Taste and adjust the seasoning as needed.

VEGETARIAN MAIN DISHES

Nearly all of these flavorful vegetarian entrees can be prepared with added meat to satisfy omnivores.

Cooking Spring Vegetables

GREEN CANELONI

A bunch of giggling celebrities made this one morning on the Today Show. The gigantic pasta tubes fill themselves. It's bound to impress your friends. Use a red sauce like Ragu or make your own sauce with four cups chopped home grown tomatoes and lots of spices. Greens can be spinach, chard, bok choi, collards, etc. Oven at 325F

2 cups chopped, packed fresh greens
3 cloves garlic, minced
1/4 cup olive oil
3 cups prepared spaghetti sauce
10 or 12 giant cannelloni
1 cup grated mozzarella or jack cheese

Chop raw greens into one-inch bits. In a deep oven proof pot, sauté garlic and greens in the oil, turning them frequently until greens are wilted. Add the tomato sauce, mix well and turn off heat.

Push caneloni, like a crowd of hollow logs, vertically into the sauce in the deep pot. The sauce will migrate up inside to fill them. Sprinkle grated cheese on top. Cover and bake 30 minutes. For the deluxe version,
add 1/2 cup cream to the grated cheese and spoon this on top.

JAPANESE VEGETABLE TEMPURA

A fun way to serve broccoli, cauliflower, carrot, green beans, zucchini, kohlrabi, bell pepper, winter squash, mushrooms, etc. Popular seafoods can be cooked as tempura too. Try shrimp, squid, or firm fish.

   Vegetables:
2-1/2 cups vegetable, in small chunks
2 cups oil for frying
Batter:
1 beaten egg
1 cup ice water
1 cup white flour
   Dipping sauce:
1 cup iced water
1 tablespoon dashi granules
 1/4 cup mirin (Japanese sweet wine)
 2 tablespoons soy sauce
 2 TB each: grated daikon raddish, grated peeled fresh ginger

Prepare cut up vegetables. For the batter, slowly add iced water to egg, while mixing. Iced water prevents the batter absorbing too much oil during cooking. Whisk in flour, and quickly mix, ignoring any lumps.

Dip vegetables in the batter to create a thin coating. Oil should be hot – at least 325 F for vegetables, up to 350 F for seafood. If a test drop of batter sinks halfway down in the oil then floats, it's 340 F. A candy thermo- meter comes in handy for frying.

Drop coated food in hot oil and cook until it's lightly browned. Line a platter with paper towel to absorb cooking oil and lay cooked tempura on that. Transfer cooked morsels to a clean platter and serve at once. As you eat them, dip each in the dipping sauce.

PASTA PRIMAVERA

Primavera means springtime. Use spring greens such as chard, arugula, kale or spinach to make this Italian springtime favorite.

1/2 pound fettuccine noodles
1/2 pound edible-pod peas
5 green onions and tops, chopped
2 cups packed chopped greens
3 TB olive oil
1/2 tsp each: dry oregano, rosemary, thyme
1/2 cup toasted sunflower seeds or nuts
1/4 cup minced parsley
Salt and pepper to taste
    Garnish: Grated Parmesan cheese

To a big pot, add 2 quarts water, 2 tsp salt and 1 tsp oil (to keep noodles from sticking together). When the water is boiling hard, drop in the noodles. While fettuccine cooks, put the peas in a large strainer and hold them in the boiling pasta water for one minute, so they barely cook. Cool peas under cold running water, and set aside.

In a fry pan with olive oil, sauté the onion five minutes. Add greens and stir about three minutes or until the greens barely wilt. Remove from heat, add peas and mix well. When the pasta is tender, drain it and serve topped with the vegetables. Garnish with grated Parmesan or Romano cheese.

MUSHROOM AND SPINACH PENNE

Cook penne or other large pasta in salted, oiled water until done. Meanwhile, in a large fry pan with lots of olive oil, toss minced garlic, sliced mushrooms and cleaned spinach. Cook them about three minutes then add fresh minced herbs (sage, rosemary, thyme, oregano, marjoram) and lots of Parmesan cheese. For a richer dish, add butter and let it melt. Add pasta to the fry pan with the veggies and stir well. Serve hot.

SPRING STIR FRY

Serve this over white or brown rice, or in a large bowl, mixed with cooked Asian noodles. Spring greens can include chard, kale, spinach, beet tops, etc. Five-spice gives any dish a distinctive Chinese flavor. A little sesame oil also enhances the Asian taste of a dish.

3 chopped green onions, including tops
1 cup edible-pod peas
2 cups packed chopped greens
1 cup tofu or tempeh chunks
1/4 cup canola oil
2 tsp Chinese five-spice mix
2 TB soy sauce
1/2 cup water
3 TB cornstarch

Heat oil in a large fry pan. Fry onions and peas about two minutes, then add greens and tofu or tempeh (or both). Cook until greens just wilt. Remove from heat and add five-spice and soy sauce. Dissolve cornstarch in water and mix well. Put pan back over low heat, and add the cornstarch mix to the stir-fry, to thicken and form a sauce as you stir. Serve over rice or noodles.

Using Summer Vegetables

SUMMER VEGETABLE TART

As good as a pie shell, use a square of filo or puff pastry dough and fold the four corners over the filling. Make a tart much as you would make a little pizza. Try with 2 cups chopped arugula (rocket) and one cup crumbled gorgonzola cheese. Always preheat oven for a tart, so the bottom of the crust gets well cooked. Oven at 400F

One uncooked piecrust, or filo dough
2 cups mixed greens and young vegetables
1/2 cup chopped onion
Fresh minced marjoram, thyme, sage, etc.
1 cup grated cheese
Salt and pepper to taste

Chop vegetables and arrange them on the pastry dough. Scatter onions and herbs. Distribute grated cheese, then add salt and pepper. Bake 30 to 40 minutes, or until crust is light brown and vegetables are cooked.

SUMMER TOMATO TART

Roma tomatoes are best, because they are meatier and less juicy. Or, use another variety, quarter them and remove seeds and juice. Oven at 350F

One square of prepared filo dough
1/4 cup basil pesto
7 medium Roma tomatoes, chopped
1 tsp each: salt, fresh thyme and marjoram
3/4 cup sour cream
1 cup grated gruyere cheese

Cover a pie tin with a ten to twelve inch square sheet of filo dough, leaving corners over the side. Prepare the tomatoes and toss them with the salt, thyme and marjoram. With a table knife, spread the pesto over the bottom of the crust. Lay in the tomatoes. Mix the sour cream with the gruyere and cover the tomatoes with this. Fold filo dough corners toward the center to make a partial top. Bake 40 minutes or until pastry is lightly browned. Serve hot.

CARROT TART

The filling is basically carrot custard. The tastier the carrots, the better the tart will be. Fresh, local organic vegetables yield superior flavor every time. Oven at 350F

A baked pie shell or filo dough.
1 beaten egg, plus one tsp water
    Filling:
1 pound thin-sliced fresh carrots
4 TB butter
1/2 cup water
1 tsp each: sugar, fresh parsley, marjoram
1/2 tsp each: salt and pepper
4 beaten eggs
1/2 cup grated mozzarella
1/2 cup grated Parmesan or Romano cheese

In a saucepan simmer covered: carrots with butter, water, herbs, salt and pepper about 15 minutes or until tender. Drain water off. Puree the mixture. Add eggs and cheeses, stirring to mix well. Pour this into the pie shell. Decorate the top with strips of dough or filo. With a pastry brush, coat the crust with the egg and water mix so it gets shiny and brown. Bake about 30 minutes or until filling sets. Cool 10 minutes before serving.

MARINARA SAUCE

This spaghetti sauce, in the style of Naples, can be used on spaghetti or pizza, in calzone or lasagna, or over polenta. Add cooked ground meat if you like. Nutmeg and sugar will soften the sharp acidity of the tomatoes.

2 medium onions, chopped
1 bell pepper, chopped
5 cloves garlic, minced
1/4 cup olive oil
6 cups chopped tomatoes
2 anchovy fillets, minced
1 tsp each: fresh oregano and thyme
1/2 tsp each: sugar and nutmeg

Sauté onions, bell pepper and garlic in the oil about five minutes. Add all the other ingredients. Simmer at least an hour, over low heat. Serve over pasta or polenta, or use to make another dish.

GARDEN VEGETABLE CALZONE

Calzone means shoe -- a hot pocket of dough with a hearty filling. Make the dough first (see basic yeast dough, below), as it needs to rise. The mix of vegetables can include summer squash, broccoli, kale, chard, kohlrabi, etc. Use a marinara sauce you made or bought. To create cheesy green-filled calzones, mix 1/2 cup pesto with 2 cups ricotta cheese and fill two calzones with this. Oven at 350F

Use Basic PIZZA Dough for the shell
    Filling:
3 cups chopped garden vegetables
1/2 cup chopped onions
4 cloves garlic, minced
1/4 cup olive oil
1 cup marinara sauce
2 TB flour (makes filling less runny)
8 oz protein (meat or tempeh)
1/2 tsp each: salt, dry rosemary, sage, oregano, nutmeg
1 cup grated jack or mozzarella cheese

Sauté onions and vegetables in oil until they are soft. Add the other filling ingredients, except the cheese, and mix together. Simmer 10 minutes. Add the cheese to the filling. Shape portions of dough into flat rounds about 8 inches across.

Lay in a generous amount of filling on one half, then fold over the other half of the dough to make a cover. Pinch around the edges to seal it tight. Poke a few vent holes. Lift with a pancake turner onto a cookie sheet. Bake 40 minutes or until the crust begins to brown.

INDIAN PAKORAS

Pakoras are spicy, vegetable puffs with a batter coating made with chickpea (garbanzo) flour. Use a variety of vegetables. Pakoras made with cauliflower and with potato slices are very popular in India. Also try zucchini chunks, asparagus tips, bell pepper squares, whole mushrooms, chopped spinach or other greens, winter squash or pumpkin chunks.

Filling:
3 cups fresh vegetables, cut into thin chunks
Batter:
2/3 cup chickpea (garbanzo) flour
2/3 cup white flour
1 tsp baking powder
1/2 tsp salt
1 tsp each: curry, dry oregano, cumin
Salt and cayenne pepper to taste
Water to make a thick creamy batter
1/2 cup olive oil

Mix flours, baking powder, salt and spices. Add water slowly, mixing well, until batter is like thick cream. Heat oil in a fry pan. Dip vegetables chunks in batter to fully coat them. Fry until they are golden. Serve hot with a chutney or relish dip.

CABBAGE PIEROGI

That's Pierozki z Kapusty in Poland, little filled dumplings cooked in water. These are time consuming, but a fun vegetarian meal, especially if children join the action.

Dough:
2 eggs, beaten
3 cups flour
1/4 tsp salt
Water as needed
Filling:
1/4 of a large cabbage
1 cup ricotta or dry cottage cheese
1 onion, minced
2 TB melted butter
Salt and pepper to taste

Shred cabbage then simmer it about ten minutes, and drain off water. Mix it with cottage cheese, onion, melted butter, salt and pepper. While the cabbage cooks, make the dough. Mix eggs, flour, salt and add just enough water that you can work it. Roll out the dough until it is thin. Cut 3-inch squares. In the center of each put a heaping tablespoon of filling. Wet the edges and fold over, pinching into a triangle. Drop into boiling salted water. When they float, they are ready. Remove with a slotted spoon. Serve hot.

STUFFED BELL PEPPERS

Our mother made stuffed peppers often, but they were off my radar until my sister Lynda served them recently. Oven at 325F

4 medium bell peppers
1/4 cup chopped green onion or shallot
2 cloves garlic, minced
2 TB olive oil
1/2 cup chopped tomato
1/2 cup chopped zucchini
1 cup cooked rice
1/2 tsp each: rosemary, oregano or marjoram
1/4 tsp each: nutmeg, sugar
1/2 cup grated Parmesan or similar cheese
Optional: chopped walnuts

Halve peppers, clean them out and set aside.
Sauté onion and garlic in oil. Add tomato and zucchini. Cook until vegetables are soft. Mix cooked vegetables, herbs, spices, rice. Heap peppers with the mix. Sprinkle tops with grated Parmesan. Place filled peppers in an oiled baking pan and bake 20 minutes. Serve hot.

SYBIL'S SPANISH RICE

1-1/2 cup dry white rice
4 cloves garlic, minced
1/3 cup olive oil
3 cups hot stock
3 chopped tomatoes
1/2 cup chopped fresh parsley
3 fresh basil leaves, chopped
1 tsp paprika
Salt and pepper to taste

Prepare the vegetables and spices to add later. Sauté raw rice and garlic in oil three minutes. Add hot stock slowly, while stirring. Cover the pan and cook on low heat 15 minutes or until stock is absorbed. Allow rice to cool five minutes then add all other ingredients. Mix well. Serve hot.

WILD RICE PILAF

Mix some wild with brown rice for flavor. Simmer 45 minutes, it then mix with some or all of these in various quantities:

Golden raisins, dried cranberries
Red bell peppers, chopped
Green onions or scallions, chopped
Chopped roasted hazelnuts
A little olive oil to moisten
Your choice of fresh herbs
Salt and pepper to taste

Re-warm the pilaf and serve hot. Keeps 5 days.

WALNUT PILAF

Grains, such as rice or wheat, with seeds such as beans or nuts, compliment each other perfectly, to provide all 21 amino acids we need for complete protein in our diets, without animal food. For variety, add chopped mushrooms, celery or bell pepper, a bit of saffron, orange zest, dill or a dash of cinnamon. Cooks, from Armenia to Zanzibar, create their own versions of pilaf. Some include lentils. A cup of chopped greens, sauted with the nuts, adds color and substance.

1-1/2 cup dry rice
3 cups stock
1/2 cup walnuts, chopped
4 cloves garlic, minced
1/2 cup green onions, chopped
3 TB canola oil
1 tsp each: thyme, sage
Salt and hot pepper to taste
1/2 cup raisins or chopped dried fruit

Cook the rice with the stock, in a covered pot, 15 minutes, or 45 minutes for brown rice. In a fry pan, sauté walnuts, garlic, onions, herbs, salt and pepper, in the oil until onions are soft. When rice is done, add it and the dry fruit to the fry pan and mix. Serve hot.

GREEN BEANS WITH GRAIN

Use summer's bounty of green beans, pre-cooked grain.

2 cups pre-cooked grain
3 TB canola oil
1/2 cup thin sliced onion
30 to 35 green beans cut to one inch
1 cup diced tomatoes
1/2 carrot, grated
2 TB cider vinegar
Salt and cayenne pepper to taste

Sauté onion in 2 TB oil until it turns golden. Add green beans, tomato, carrot, vinegar, salt and pepper. Mix and simmer 20 minutes, allowing some of the liquid to evaporate. To another fry pan, add remaining oil and cooked grain. Stir-fry until grain begins to brown. Form grain into a ring around the outside of a platter. Fill the center of the ring with the green bean mix. Serve hot.

TABBOULI

A hearty cold dish, serious tabouli is loaded with fresh parsley and mint, and lighter on the grain. It is popular in countries of the eastern Mediterranean. We often make tabouli using cooked quinoa instead of bulgur.

1 cup bulgur wheat (or quinoa)
2 cups boiling water
1 cup minced parsley
1/2 cup grated carrot
1/4 cup chopped green onions
1/4 cup minced fresh mint
1/3 cup lemon juice
1/4 cup olive oil
Salt and pepper to taste
    Optional: 1/2 cup raisins or cucumber or tomatoes

Pour boiling water over dry bulgur, cover and let stand 15 minutes or until the water is all absorbed. (Quinoa has to cook 15 minutes.) Cool grain, then mix with other ingredients. Serve at room temperature or chilled.

Enjoying Fall Vegetables

PUMPKIN MASALA

In India, a masala is a mix of spices. Try this tasty way to enjoy pumpkin or winter squash. It's good without the hot.

1 onion, chopped
5 cloves garlic, minced
1 tsp each: honey or sugar, hot pepper
2 TB curry powder
1/4 cup olive oil or ghee (clarified butter)
3 chopped tomatoes, or one 13 oz can
1-1/2 to 2 pounds pumpkin or winter squash
  Garnish: Lemon or lime wedges, roasted sunflower seeds

Steam or microwave the pumpkin until it is soft, then peel and cut it into chunks. In the oil or ghee, over medium heat, fry onion, garlic and spices until onion is soft. Add tomatoes and pumpkin and one cup of water. Cover and simmer 10 minutes.

Serve in bowls with a squeeze of lemon or lime juice and lots of sunflower seeds. Good with brown rice or flat bread, and a salad.

MOROCCAN VEGETABLE STEW

In this hearty North African favorite, high protein, canned garbanzos (chick peas) are easy and fast. Use canned tomatoes in winter. Tomatoes are higher in anti-cancer lycopene after cooking, but their Vitamin C is destroyed by heat.

1/4 cup olive oil
1 small onion, chopped
3 cloves garlic, minced
2 cups cooked garbanzos
2 tomatoes, chopped
2 potatoes, chopped
2 carrots, thin sliced
3 TB minced parsley
1 cup peeled and diced winter squash
1 tsp each: cumin, ginger, tumeric, salt
Hot pepper to taste

In a large pot, sauté onion and garlic in oil. Add other ingredients. Cover and simmer 45 minutes. Traditionally served with couscous, this stew is good with rice or artisan bread and a green salad.

POLENTA WITH FALL MUSHROOMS

Easy to make, polenta is good with a wide variety of toppings. Less water for stiffer, more for a softer result .

    Basic polenta:
2/3 cup coarse ground yellow corn meal
2 cups stock or salted water
2 TB butter
    Mushroom topping:
2 cups sliced fresh mushrooms
1/4 cup olive oil
1/4 cup diced onions
1/2 cup thin sliced carrot
1/2 cup thin sliced parsnips
1 TB dark soy sauce
2 TB flour
1/2 cup cream
        Garnish: Toasted nuts

Start by mixing the corn meal into cold stock or water, in a heavy pot, since it burns easily. Heat slowly, while stirring. Continue stirring while it simmers for five minutes. Cover and remove from heat. Leave it for fifteen minutes or until all the liquid is absorbed. Or cook 90 minutes in double boiler, stirring occasionally.

Serve hot and soft, in bowls. Or cool it to harden, then cut into wedges and warm to serve.

Sauté vegetables in oil until all are soft. Add soy sauce and mix well, then toss with flour. Slowly add cream as the mixture thickens. Serve hot over warm polenta.

LEEK AND SPINACH PIE

Make your own double pie crust, or use filo dough. Fill the unbaked shell then cover with a second crust. Cut several vents in top to release steam. Oven at 350F

Filo or a prepared uncooked piecrust
Filling:
1 large bunch of spinach
1 cup chopped onions
2 cups chopped white parts of leeks
10 green onions, chopped
1 tsp each: fresh dill, parsley
2 large eggs, beaten
4 oz feta cheese, crumbled
Salt and pepper to taste

Clean and chop spinach and sprinkle generously with salt, then let it stand 20 minutes. Chop the other vegetables. Sauté onions, green onions and leeks in the oil until they soften.

Now, use your hands to squeeze as much water as you can from the spinach, so the pie will not be too watery. Mix spinach with sauted items, eggs, feta, and pepper. No more salt is needed. Fill the filo or crust with the vegetable mixture.

Add another layer of pastry on top. Trim the edges. Cut vents in crust to let steam out. Brush with a little olive oil to moisten. Bake 45 minutes or until the crust is light brown.

CYPRUS VEGETABLE STEW

Here's another version of the Mediterranean garbanzo and vegetable stew to make in fall or winter, excellent with rice or crusty bread.

1/4 cup olive oil
1 onion diced
4 cloves garlic, minced
4 cups chard or seasonal greens
2 cups chopped fresh or canned tomatoes
2 cups garbanzos (chick peas)
Salt and hot chiles to taste
    Garnish: 1/2 cup crumbled feta cheese

Sauté onion and garlic in oil. Add greens and stir as they wilt. Add tomatoes, garbanzos, salt and hot pepper. Cover and simmer 20 minutes. Serve over rice or in bowls, topped with crumbled feta cheese.

FALL MUSHROOMS ON TOAST

Our dad liked creamed mushrooms on toast for breakfast, on some Saturdays well before dawn, so that by the time the sun rose we could be out on the ocean fishing from his little boat. Try them for lunch or supper.

2 cups mushrooms, sliced
4 TB butter
1 TB of flour
1 cup of cream
1 TB Worcestershire sauce
Salt and pepper to taste

Over medium heat, cook mushrooms in butter until they absorb most of their juices. Add flour and mix it in, then slowly add cream as it thickens, then other ingredients. Serve hot, over toast.

FALL MUSHROOM RISOTTO

Brown rice CAN cook in 15 minutes, like white rice, but only if you soak it in water or stock for two hours before cooking. Otherwise, brown rice takes 45 minutes.

1/2 cup chopped onion
3 cloves garlic, minced
1/4 cup olive oil
1 pound fresh mushrooms, sliced
1 TB each: fresh rosemary and thyme
1 cup of rice
2-1/2 cups of stock
3 TB of red wine
1/4 cup each: minced parsley, minced mint
Salt and pepper to taste

Garnish: Fresh grated Parmesan or Romano cheese.

Sauté onion and garlic in oil five minutes. Add mushrooms, herbs and dry rice and stir for about three minutes. Slowly add the stock as you continue to stir until the rice is cooked, about 15 minutes. This treatment makes the rice creamy. If you get tired of stirring, just cover the pan and it will steam. Remove from heat and add the wine, parsley, mint, salt and pepper. Serve hot.

PUMPKIN DUMPLINGS (GNOCCHI DI ZUCCA)

Zucca means squash or pumpkin in Italian, and zucchini are the little ones, "ini" being the diminutive ending. Gnocchi is pronounced N yo kee.

This recipe uses pumpkin or any winter squash. Using a small can of pumpkin is not cheating.

2 cups cooked pumpkin puree
2 eggs, beaten
2 cups flour
1/2 tsp each: baking powder, salt, garlic, nutmeg

Mince garlic. Mix all ingredients. Let the mix stand 30 minutes. Boil 2 quarts of water. Stir batter again and drop spoonfuls into the boiling water. When they float, they are ready.

Remove them with a slotted spoon. Serve with butter or savory sauce, as a side dish or centerpiece of a small meal.

FETTUCCINI, WILD MUSHROOMS AND CREAM

Chanterelles, pale orange cones with gills part way down the stem, are perfect for this dish, but it's excellent with almost any mild variety, including those found in stores.

To make crème fraiche use one cup of heavy cream. Add two tablespoons of yogurt or buttermilk and leave on the counter overnight, with a cloth cover. Various pastas suffice. Fettucini is ideal.

1 pound fresh (or 8 ounces dry) fettucini
2 pounds fresh mushrooms, sliced
4 cups stock
1 cup crème fraiche
3 TB soy sauce
Salt and pepper
1/2 cup minced fresh parsley

Boil a large pot of water, add salt and a bit of oil and drop in the noodles. While the noodle water heats, boil the stock in a large fry pan. Drop in the mushrooms and continue boiling, without a cover, to reduce the liquid to half. Reduce the heat and add the crème fraiche. Add soy sauce, which gives a rich brown color. Add salt and pepper, as needed, then the parsley. Drain the noodles and toss with the sauce. Serve hot

Winter Veggie Dishes

WINTER GREENS AND FRIED RICE

Chard, kale, collards, bok choi, cabbage or almost any other greens can be prepared this way.

3 to 4 cups packed greens
1/2 cup carrot, thin sliced
2 TB oil
1 beaten egg
2 cups cooked rice
Salt and pepper to taste
    Garnish: 1/4 cup chopped green onions

Clean the greens and chop small. (Use stems in soup later.) Sauté the carrot in 1 TB of oil, then add the greens and stir as they wilt. In a separate fry pan, sauté the cooked rice in 2 TB oil, then add the egg and scramble it, breaking rice and egg mix into crumbles. Add the vegetables. salt and pepper. Mix well. Serve hot topped with chopped green onions.

ROOT VEGETABLE TART

Not quick, but easy and good enough for company, the tarts use a basic piecrust. Individual tarts are filled with vegetables that are plentiful in the dark of the year, then topped with good feta cheese. Oven at 350F

    Crust:
Filo dough or a single piecrust
    Filling:
2 cups winter veggies – onion, parsnip, turnip, carrot, beets, rutabaga, etc.
1/4 cup olive oil
1 TB fresh rosemary, minced
Salt and pepper to taste
1/2 cup crumbled feta or goat cheese
2 tsp balsamic vinegar
3 cloves garlic, smashed and minced
2 TB (more) of olive oil
    Garnish: 4 whole sprigs fresh rosemary

Peel and slice vegetables. In a large fry pan, sauté vegetables with oil, rosemary, salt and pepper about five minutes, then add a little water and steam them about 15 minutes or until all are soft.

Meanwhile, divide piecrust or filo and roll out four equal rounds. Lay these rounds, well separated, on a cookie sheet, ready for filling. When the vegetables are nicely done, lift them with a slotted spoon into a bowl and toss with cheese and garlic. Distribute this filling to the four rounds, leaving a border about an inch wide. Turn up the borders to form shallow bowls around the vegetables. Bake the filled rounds 20 minutes or until shell is golden. Serve hot, drizzled with a little more olive oil, each garnished with a sprig of fresh rosemary.

ELEGANT CAULIFLOWER

Cauliflower is sweetest in the winter. Use a whole one here, about 8 inches in diameter. Adding the eggs and cheese turns this delicate vegetable into a luncheon meal or impressive dish for dinner.

1 whole cauliflower, trimmed and cored
4 eggs, beaten
1/2 cup grated cheese
1 tsp dill
1/2 tsp salt, pepper to taste
1/2 cup milk

Steam the whole cauliflower until tender. While it cooks, beat eggs and grate cheese. Mix them together, add dill, salt and milk. Transfer whole cooked cauliflower to an ovenproof bowl and pour the egg mixture over it, so it pools around the sides. Cover and microwave four minutes or bake 20 minutes, until the egg is set. For the very similar Cavalfiore alla Romana, served in Rome, cut the cauliflower into chunks and line the baking dish with a layer of breadcrumbs or dry bread cubes, then lay the cauliflower etc. on top of those.

CRANBERRY AND PEAR STUFFING

Though it makes a nice vegetarian dish, you can use this stuffing with a big bird too.

4 cups cubed French baguette bread
1 pear, cored and diced
1 tart apple, cored and diced
1 cup dried cranberries
1 onion, chopped
1 cup chopped walnuts
1 TB each: salt, pepper, nutmeg, parsley, rosemary, sage
1 cup red wine
3 cups stock

Toss bread, pear, apple, cranberry, onion and nuts with the seasonings in a large casserole. Mix wine and stock and pour over the dry mixture. Bake one hour.

HAZELNUT POLENTA

The chopped nuts in the coating make this a rich and flavorful main dish.

3 cups stock or water
1 cup of medium grind yellow corn meal
1/2 tsp each: salt, paprika, thyme, rosemary
2 TB butter
1/2 cup grated cheese
2 eggs, beaten
1 cup finely chopped roasted hazelnuts
1 cup of raw wheat germ or fine bread crumbs
Olive oil for frying
   Garnish: Mix sour cream or plain yogurt with minced green onions or chives

Stir cornmeal, spices and butter into cool stock as it heats. Simmer the mix, while stirring often, for about 10 minutes, until it is thick. Or cook 90 minutes in a double boiler. Add grated cheese and mix well. Pour the mixture into a flat pan and cool in the refrigerator until it hardens (1 hour).

Cut the hardened polenta into diamonds. Dip each piece in the egg batter, then the chopped nuts, then the wheat germ or bread crumbs to create a coating on both sides. Fry until both sides brown. Serve with sour cream garnish.

SCOTTISH BARLEY RISOTTO

Risotto is officially made with rice but barley thrives here and grows well in Scotland, where the climate is too chilly and wet for wheat or rice. For variety, stir in 2 TB of lemon juice before serving. Oven at 325F

3 cups stock
1 cup sliced mushrooms
1/2 stick butter
1 onion, diced
2 cloves garlic, minced
2 cups dry pearl barley
Salt and pepper to taste
    Garnish: Minced parsley, grated cheese

Warm stock until it's steaming. Add mushrooms, cover and remove from heat. In a heavy fry pan, over low heat, sauté onions and garlic in the butter until soft. Add dry barley and stir to coat with the butter. Add mushrooms in stock, salt and pepper. Bring to a boil, then cover and bake about 35 minutes. Serve hot, sprinkled with minced parsley and grated cheese.

POULTRY AND MEAT

A few chickens, raised the old way, can run loose and turn garden waste and nuisance bugs into tasty, high quality protein. In drier parts of Oregon and much of the rest of the world, climate and soil conditions make it difficult to grow crops but practical to keep chickens or graze.

While consuming less fatty meat reduces the probability of many diseases, a rigid vegan diet is asking for malnutrition and depression. All the evidence points to our ancestors being aggressive hunters and clever herders and animal breeders.

We know that numerous health problems result not from meat itself but from eating far too much of it and eating meat raised in unnatural ways so that it is no longer the product it used to be. Small amounts of good meat, eggs, dairy and animal fat will not cause heart disease or any other illness. The China Study, by nutritionists and biochemists from Oxford, Cornell and Beijing Universities, over 30 years and more than 600,000 people shows that people who keep animal products, including eggs and dairy, to under 20% of calories have near zero incidence of the "diseases of affluence" including cancer, heart disease, and diabetes.

Most animal products sold here come to us through factory farming operations. The vast majority of America's beef comes from range cattle purchased from ranchers and taken to feedlots for fattening. A meat packer told me that people demand soft, fatty meat, so the industry is simply catering to taste. At feedlots, tens of thousands of cattle stand crowded together in manure up to their ankles or knees. Cattle digestion is set up for grass. At feedlots they get corn that adds fat but makes them sick, and could better be used to feed people. To survive feedlot conditions, cattle require large amounts of antibiotics. And mass production, fast action slaughterhouses make very ugly mistakes.

Most of our pork now comes from smaller but equally unnatural operations where hundreds of young pigs fill a concrete floored structure and food is distributed by big machines. The filthy runoff pollutes ground water and streams, over large areas. Industrial poultry production is equally sad for the animals, with several chickens in each tiny cage inside a huge barn with tens of thousands of others, whole lives spent indoors.

Industrial meat operations are hard on land, unhealthy for animals and produce food with compromised nutritional value because soil is worn out. Some small farmers go this route, but only corporations get rich. Another good reason to choose local, traditionally raised meat is that animal foods, far more than plant foods, concentrate toxins and chemical additives.

If you aren't going to go totally organic, it's smart to at least go organic in the meat, eggs and dairy department. If you want to save money, buy the cheaper cuts but from healthier animals. When you do, ask for those bones that make such good stock. Or buy from local custom meat cutters.

Cooking Poultry

STUFFING A TURKEY, GLUTEN FREE

Tasty and easy, I invented this rice stuffing when we were short on bread, years before anyone avoided gluten.

2 cups brown rice
1/2 cup wild rice
5 cups stock
2 cups chopped celery
1 large onion, chopped
1 TB each: basil, oregano, thyme, garlic powder
1 quart canned apricots, drained and chopped
Salt and pepper to taste

Simmer rice in stock 45 minutes, until all the liquid is absorbed. Cool then mix in other ingredients, adding a little apricot juice to make it moister, more salt and pepper if needed. Stuff the mixture into the bird's cavities, extra in a casserole pan. Partway through baking the bird, use juices in the bottom of the pan to moisten stuffing in the casserole, then cover and bake it the last hour of turkey baking.

ITALIAN CHICKEN CASSEROLE

When you have leftover turkey or chicken this makes an easy meal, good with hearty bread and a green salad. Oven at 425F

5 cloves garlic, minced
1/2 cup pancetta ham or smoked bacon
2 cups cooked white beans
2 cups cooked chicken chunks
1 cup each chopped: steamed onions, carrots and red peppers

Sauté garlic with chopped ham or bacon. Put it in the bottom of a large baking dish. Layer in the beans and chicken, then vegetables. Bake 20 minutes.

TURKEY CREOLE WITH RICE

Use turkey, leftover or fresh, or chicken or other meats. Double this recipe and enjoy a few days later. Use fresh or canned tomatoes.

3 cups pre-cooked rice
1/4 cup olive oil
1 onion, chopped
1 bell pepper, chopped
1 pound turkey breast
4 cloves garlic, minced
2 cups chopped tomatoes
1 tsp each: salt, dry oregano, dry rosemary
1 bay leaf
Cayenne pepper to taste
2 TB flour

Cook the rice and keep it warm. Sauté the onion, pepper and garlic in oil. Cut turkey into chunks and add along with tomatoes and seasoning. Cover and simmer 45 minutes. Remove the bay leaf. Mix the flour with a little water and add this paste to juices to thicken them as they continue to cook a bit longer. Serve over rice, with salad.

DUCK WITH QUINCE

Have no quince? Make this dish with one large tart apple. Quinces are much too sour to eat raw but lend excitement to a fatty roast duck. Choose the largest of the yellow-green fruit with no blemishes. This dish has several steps but it's not difficult. And a good duck it definitely worth the effort.

2/3 cup red wine
1/2 cup stock
6 dried figs
1 duck breast, about 2 pounds
2 medium quinces
1 firm-ripe pear, such as Bosc
Salt and pepper to taste
2 tablespoons minced shallots
1 teaspoon balsamic vinegar

Cut figs in quarters. Simmer wine, stock and figs until the liquid is reduced to about 1/2 cup. Set aside for sauce.

While the stock cooks down, cut the fat and skin from the duck and sauté it about ten minutes to render out the liquid fat you'll use. Toss the skin. Sprinkle duck breasts with salt and pepper. Fry breasts in the duck fat until both sides brown, then reduce heat and cook three minutes more or until the center loses its pink color. Put breasts on a platter in a warm oven.

Peel and core the quinces and pear. Slice them about 1/3 inch thick, then salt and pepper them. Put sliced shallots and quince into the duck fat and sauté them for about 2 minutes. Add the pears and continue to saute until the quince and pears are tender when pierced with a fork. Remove the fruit to the warm oven.

Now the sauce... Pour the stock and fig mixture into the pan with duck fat, scraping up any clinging bits. Cook to reduced to about 1/3 cup. Stir in the balsamic vinegar at the end.

Take the duck and the fruit out of the oven. Cut the duck into 1/2-inch-thick slices and arrange on a platter. Surround with the quince, pears and figs, then drizzle sauce over all.

CHICKEN CACCIATORE

By cooking ingredients separately, you develop each to its maximum potential. This zesty Italian dish has long been an American favorite, a grand way to enjoy chicken. Use fresh or canned tomatoes.

4 chicken breast halves
1/2 cup olive oil
2 medium onions, sliced
2 cloves garlic, minced
3 bell peppers, sliced
1/2 cup red wine
4 cups chopped tomatoes
1 tsp each: dry oregano, rosemary, sage
1/2 tsp each: nutmeg, cinnamon
2 cups sliced mushrooms
1 TB of butter
Salt and pepper to taste

In a large fry pan, ideally cast iron, sauté chicken in oil until the outside begins to brown, about five minutes. Remove and set aside. In the same oil, sauté onion, garlic and pepper. Remove with a slotted spoon and set aside. To the same pan add red wine, tomatoes and seasonings.

With a metal spatula, scrape the tasty glazing off the pan, helped by the acids you've just added. Cook three minutes. Add the chicken, onion and pepper mix. Cover and simmer 20 minutes. While the chicken cooks, sauté the mushrooms in butter until they start to brown. Just before serving, add them to the chicken pan. Good over pasta, with crusty bread and salad.

UMPQUA RIVER COQ AU VIN (Chicken in wine)

Modified for the Northwest, this dish is even better a day later, so it's a good one to make ahead for guests. If you have a plum tree, split and dry some of your harvest.

1 whole chicken, cut up
1/4 cup olive oil
1 onion, thin sliced
4 cloves garlic, minced
3 carrots, sliced
2 cups pitted prunes
2 cups dry red wine
1 tsp each: dry rosemary, basil and thyme
2 cups sliced mushrooms
Salt and pepper to taste

In a heavy pot over high heat, brown the chicken pieces in half the oil. In a fry pan, in remaining oil, sauté onion, garlic and carrots with salt and pepper. Add these to the chicken pot. Add prunes, wine and herbs. Cover, simmer 45 minutes. Add mushrooms and cook ten minutes more.

IRISH CHICKEN CASSEROLE

1 cut up chicken, about 4 pounds
4 slices bacon, cut to one inch
2 cups chopped onion
2 cups thin-sliced carrots
1 tsp each: fresh thyme and sage
3 cups stock
Salt and pepper to taste
3 TB flour

In a deep pot, sauté the bacon until it's crisp. Remove it from the pot and in the bacon fat brown the chicken pieces. Return the bacon to the chicken pot and add onions, carrots, thyme, stock, salt and pepper. Simmer one hour. If you're adding mushrooms, do it at this point.

Near the end, dip out one-half cup of cooking liquid and let it cool. In a small bowl, mix this warm liquid into the 3 TB flour to form a paste. Add this back to the pot, mix it in and reheat to thicken juices. Serve with rice or potatoes.

POULE AU POT

This chicken and veggie pot roast will make even factory farmed chicken taste pretty good.

4-pound chicken, whole
3 chopped onions
3 chopped carrots
2 peeled and chopped turnips
1 cup packed chard, chopped
1 tsp each: dry thyme, sage, mustard
3 cloves fresh minced garlic
1/4 cup chopped parsley
Salt and pepper to taste
1 cup white wine
3 cups chicken or vegetable soup stock

Make a stuffing of uncooked chopped vegetables, herbs, salt and pepper and fill as much of the body cavity of the chicken as you can. Place the chicken in a large pot, pour stock and wine around it then add remaining stuffing mix to the liquid.

Cover and simmer one hour, adding water if needed. Cut up the chicken in the kitchen or serve the whole chicken on a platter, to be carved. Good with rice or mashed potatoes, and a green salad. Thanks to Virginia Slate for testing and upgrading the seasonings for this dish.

CHICKEN PAPRIKASH

Hungary grows hundreds of varieties of the fruits we call peppers, a national favorite there. Paprika is made from dried mild peppers, and they use a lot of it.

1 cut up chicken
1 tsp salt
4 TB butter
1 diced onion
3 TB paprika
1/4 tsp cloves
1 cup water or stock
1 TB flour
1 tsp paprika
4 servings of cooked wide noodles

Pat chicken pieces dry and sprinkle with salt. In a large fry pan, sauté the onions in butter until soft. Add 3 TB paprika and cloves, and mix well to coat onions. Lay chicken pieces in the pan and add the water or stock. Cover and simmer 45 minutes, stirring about every ten minutes and adding water if needed. Near the end of cooking, mix sour cream, flour and 1 tsp paprika. Add this to the chicken. Cook uncovered about five minutes. Serve over a bed of cooked wide noodles or Hungarian pasta, called Tarhonya.

TARHONYA NOODLES

Hungarian pasta is usually served with meat dishes, so it's included it here, as you might want to serve foods in this section with Tarhonya.

Add flour to one beaten egg to form a work-able dough. Knead dough until it's smooth and flexible. Grate this on the large holes of a hand grater or press it through a wide-mesh sieve. Cook it fresh or allow it to dry. To cook, sauté it in meat fat, then boil it in salted water as with any other pasta. It can also be used in stews, soup, stuffing or as a side dish. Kids love it with cheese.

Red Meat Dishes

AFGHAN WINTER SQUASH WITH MEAT SAUCE

2 to 3 pounds cooked winter squash
2 cups ground meat (lamb is most authentic)
3 TB olive oil
1 cup chopped onion
2 cups chopped tomatoes
2 TB honey
1 tsp each: cinnamon, thyme, sage, rosemary
Salt to taste
   Garnish: 1 cup plain yogurt

Open squash and remove seeds and fibers. Bake or microwave squash until soft. While it cooks, make a ground meat sauce. Fry meat in oil with onions. Add chopped tomatoes, honey, spices and salt. Cook uncovered over low heat for about 15 minutes. Cut squash into serving-sized chunks. Serve in shallow soup plates, a bed of squash topped with meat sauce, garnished with yogurt. In a pinch, you can use spaghetti sauce with meat.

PORK HAZELNUT TERRINE

Baked in a loaf pan, most terrines are best when chilled for several days then sliced thin as an appetizer or quick meal. Oven at 300F

2 pounds plain ground pork
1 large onion, chopped
1/2 tsp each: nutmeg, black pepper
1 tsp each: dry marjoram, thyme, sage
1 TB salt
1/4 cup red wine
2 beaten eggs
1 cup chopped roasted hazelnuts
3 bay leaves
3 strips of thick bacon

In a large bowl, use clean hands to mix the pork, onion, spices, salt, wine and beaten eggs. In the bottom of a loaf pan place the two bay leaves, and on top of them the three strips of bacon. Fill the pan with the meat mixture and shape it with your hands. Cover the loaf pan tightly with foil. Bake 2-1/2 hours. Without lifting the foil, cool two hours then put in the refrigerator for two days. Serve with crusty bread and spicy mustard.

SAUSAGE ZUCCHINI BOATS

Chris Hazen made these at a student co-op in Eugene. Use any zucchini at least 10 inches long. This is the best way I know to use those that get lost under the big leaves until they've outgrown their welcome and become rather starchy. AKA: zook canoes. Oven at 375F

2 overgrown zucchinis
1/4 cup olive oil
1 cup cooked rice
1 cup cooked spicy pork sausage
2 chopped tomatoes
2 TB minced parsley
2 cloves garlic, minced
1 TB thyme

Split the zucchinis the long way. Scoop seeds out and discard them. Spoon out about half the remaining squash meat, chop it and put it into a large frying pan with the oil and other ingredients. Mix well, cover and cook over low heat about ten minutes. Load this sauce into the hollow boats. Lay filled boats on a cookie sheet and bake 45 minutes.

IRISH WHITE LAMB STEW

The more typical Irish lamb stew included colorful carrots, and is made the same way. Oven at 300F

2 pounds of lamb, diced
4 medium potatoes, in chunks
3 medium onions, in chunks
1 tsp each: dry thyme and rosemary
1 bay leaf
2 cups water
Salt and pepper to taste

In a large casserole, layer in lamb, potatoes, then onions, sprinkling salt, pepper, thyme and rosemary over each layer. Add the bay leaf. Pour in water. Bake two hours or until potatoes are soft.

FAJITAS (Fa HEE tas)

With Mexican fillings brought to the table still sizzling, fajitas fulfill their promise as we load hot spicy pork or beef and vegetables into warm tortillas, then drizzle with sauce.

8 medium or 4 large tortillas
1 onion, sliced thick
1 bell pepper, long slices
1 cup of thin-sliced chard or kale
1 pound of pork or chicken breast
1/4 cup olive oil
2 tsp cumin
2 tsp chili powder
Salt and pepper to taste
Garnishes in bowls: 1 cup sour cream,
1 cup salsa or guacamole

Cut onion, pepper and meats into pencil-like pieces. Over high heat, quickly saute vegetables and meat in oil, with condiments. Bring the hot frying pan to the table and place it on a trivet, next to a basket of warm tortillas, wrapped in a napkin.

Each diner can scoop some filling into tortillas, add sour cream and salsa, fold over and dig in. Some people like to double the tortillas and fold the bottom tight, but leakage is inevitable. Napkins required.

POTATO DISHES

The Incas of Peru bred hundreds of colorful varieties of potatoes, adapted to local growing conditions and still grown. To preserve food through a cold winter, they crushed potatoes, spread them on mats and left them out under the low-moisture freezing sky at high altitudes. That flakey powder keeps well, and was the inspiration for the modern instant potato industry.

Agro-biz potatoes carry one of the heaviest loads of chemicals. Conventional potatoes are dirt cheap, organic are expensive. It's remarkably easy to grow your own. Potatoes prefer loose soil, lots of loose mulch and manure, some compost and an occasional deep watering. In early spring, cut some in half, bury them and wait. When the vines dry up, see what treasure you can dig up -- especially fun for kids.

A medium potato is just 70 Calories. It's what you put WITH potatoes that makes them fattening. Substitute a little olive oil for some of the butter.

Stove Top Potato Dishes

EXCELLENT MASHED POTATOES

In Paris, we dined at L'Atelier de Joel Robuchon. The master chef's unforgettable bistro served small works of edible art -- delights far too elaborate to contemplate duplicating. When this international icon published his secret method for mashed potatoes, I was surprised by how easy it is.

Choose medium sized potatoes. Scrub but do not peel them. Place them in a pot of salted water, cover and simmer 25 minutes. If you choose young new potatoes, salt them at the end. They won't be gooey. Remove potatoes to the colander and let them cool, and dry. In a mixing bowl, mash them by hand. Mix in plenty of butter with a wood spoon. Add hot milk if the potatoes seem too dry. That's it. To cut the butter, substitute olive oil. Now, experiment with fresh herbs and see what pleases.

SPICY HOME FRIES

3 medium red or white potatoes, sliced
1 onion, chopped
1/4 cup olive oil
1/2 tsp each: cumin, curry, cardamom
Salt and cayenne pepper to taste

Simmer the sliced potatoes until they are barely soft. While the potatoes cook, use a big fry pan to sauté the onion in the oil. Drain the potatoes. (Save the water for stock.) Add potatoes, spices and salt to the medium-hot fry pan and turn over and over as the potatoes brown. Add oil if needed. Serve hot.

GARLIC MASH

Why consult a recipe when we all know how to make mashed potatoes? Well, who knew it really is important to cook potatoes whole, with skins on and not peeled first, if you want them to taste potato-y? Peeled first, mashed potatoes can get watery and thin. You really

need about half a stick of butter or a quarter cup of olive oil per pound for a tasty, properly textured mash.
And the butter has to be added first, not after the milk, or the result will be gooey. Per pound, add half a cup of half-and-half, not cream, not whole milk, for a light and supple decadence. Per pound, add two cloves garlic. I like to mince the garlic and add it uncooked to the mashed potatoes along with the half-and-half.

IRISH POTATO FARLS

This Ulster pan bread is quick and easy, once you've made the mashed potatoes. Scots make farls from leftover oatmeal and it's just as simple, baked or fried.

2 cups mashed potatoes
1-1/2 cup white or wheat flour
1 tsp salt
1 tsp dried parsley
1/4 cup cooking oil
1 cup water

Mix all together to form dough, adding water or flour as needed. In an 8 to 10 inch, well-oiled, cast-iron pan form one rounded, flat shape. Cover the pan to keep heat in, the cook on one side about 8 minutes, then the other, until both sides are light brown. Cut into quarters to make farls. Good with sausages and eggs.

EVELYN'S PICNIC POTATO SALAD

Since the childhood beach picnics on Lopez Island, I've enjoyed a simple potato salad. Peel russets, but no need to peel other varieties of potato for this dish.

4 medium potatoes
4 eggs
3 stalks celery, chopped with tops
1/2 cup chopped dill pickle
1/4 cup minced fresh parsley
1/2 cup mayonnaise
2 TB prepared mustard
1/4 cup vinaigrette dressing

Boil the potatoes in salty water until waxy, but not soft. Drain and cool them.

Boil eggs about 11 minutes, drop into cold water to loosen shells then slide shells off. In a large bowl combine potato chunks, and thin-sliced hard-boiled eggs. Add celery, pickle and parsley.

Make a dressing by mixing mayonnaise, mustard and vinaigrette. Add to the salad and toss to mix. Serve cold.

SALADE NICOISE

Tuna and anchovies tell you this potato salad originated near the sea. Nicoise (neese WOZ) tells you it's from Nice on the French Riviera, founded in 350 BC by sea-going Greek traders.

4 cups salad greens
2 ripe tomatoes cut in quarters
3 large potatoes, cut in chunks
16 green beans, cut in 2-inch pieces
1 can tuna, 6-1/2 ounce size, drained

    Dressing:
1 tsp each: dry mustard and basil
3 cloves garlic, minced
1/2 cup olive oil
2 TB white wine vinegar
    Garnish: 4 anchovy fillets,
8 black or green olives

Cook potatoes until waxy, but not soft, then drain and cool. Steam green beans, drain and cool. Mix dressing and toss it with tuna, potatoes and beans. Lay a bed of greens on each plate, then a scoop of potato mix. Around this, arrange slices of tomato and the olives. Over the top of potato mix, lay an anchovy fillet. There it is, the real thing.

SOUR POTATOES

The Pennsylvania Dutch (who speak German, which its speakers call Deutsch) brought this from Germany.

2 cups cooked diced potatoes
3 strips sliced bacon
1/4 cup each: chopped onion, bell pepper
1 raw egg, beaten
2 TB cider vinegar
1 tsp sugar
Salt and pepper to taste
2 hard boiled eggs, peeled and sliced
    Optional: one sliced dill pickle stirred in before the egg topping is put on.

Boil diced potatoes and set aside. Cut bacon into one-inch pieces and fry it until it curls. Remove the bacon and set aside. To the bacon fat, add onion and bell pepper, and sauté them.

Mix the raw egg with the vinegar, sugar, salt and pepper. Pour this into the pan with the onion and bell pepper and stir constantly as it thickens. Add the potatoes and cooked bacon to the pan. Serve hot.

HOT GERMAN POTATO SALAD

At beer hall restaurants in Germany, this dish typically accompanies a fat, spicy sausage and sauerkraut.

4 cups chopped potatoes
1 tsp salt
3 slices bacon, small pieces
1 cup chopped onion
1 TB flour
1/2 cup stock
1/2 cup cider vinegar
2 TB sugar
1/4 cup minced fresh parsley, or 2 TB dry

In a pot of salted water, boil potatoes until they are tender. While they cook, cut up the bacon and fry it about 3 minutes, then add onions and sauté them in the bacon fat. Add the flour and stir well, then slowly add stock as sauce thickens. Drain the potatoes. Add vinegar, sugar and potatoes to the onions and bacon. Remove from heat, stir well and add parsley. Serve hot.

GNOCCHI – POTATO DUMPLINGS

Use gnocchi (NYO kee) wherever you might use pasta. This recipe, one of dozens, is from Central Italy.

2 medium potatoes, boiled until soft
1-1/2 cups flour
1 tsp baking powder
1/2 tsp salt
1/4 tsp nutmeg

Drain, then dry, the cooked potatoes and thoroughly mash them while dry. Then add the other ingredients and mix well. Turn this dough onto a floured surface and knead like bread dough for three minutes, punching and folding. Roll dough into snakes one inch in diameter. Slice these into half-inch lengths. Press each round so your finger makes a deep hollow in the center.

Into a large pot of salted boiling water, drop the cup-like gnocchi in batches of a couple of dozen. They will sink, but rise as they cook. When all are floating, remove them with a slotted spoon and boil the next batch. Serve with spaghetti sauce or other toppings.

POLISH POTATO DUMPLINGS
Halfway between gnocchi and latkes.

3 medium potatoes, peeled and grated
2 eggs, beaten
1/4 cup olive oil
1 TB dried parsley
1 tsp each: powdered thyme, garlic, mustard
Salt and pepper to taste
1 cup flour

Put grated potatoes in the center of a cloth napkin or dishtowel and squeeze out the liquid. Add eggs, oil, herbs, salt and pepper, then slowly add flour to make a dough. Form walnut-sized balls and drop them in salted boiling water. When they float they are done. The Polish make extra, and the next day fry them in bacon fat.

PERFECT LATKES

I enjoyed helping Deborah make dozens of these latkes for her annual Hanukkah party. They are good as part of a meal, any time. Great for breakfast too, with applesauce and sour cream.

2 pounds Yukon gold or Russet potatoes
1 onion, chopped
2 large eggs, beaten
1/4 cup white flour
1/2 tsp salt, pepper to taste
2 cups canola oil
1/2 cup chopped green onion
1 cup sour cream

Peeling potatoes produces lighter colored latkes. Grate or shred potatoes into cold water so they don't darken. Leave them about 30 minutes so excess starch dissolves away. Drain off water. Place grated potatoes in a dry dishtowel. Twist the towel hard, to remove as much water as you can from the potatoes, so your latkes will be nice and crisp instead of soggy. Now, combine potatoes with onion, egg, flour, salt and pepper and mix well.

To a large fry pan, add 1/2 inch of oil. Using about 1/3 cup for each, form the mixture into round pancakes. Drop batter into hot oil. Fry until edges are browned then flip over and cook another 3 minutes or until browned. Don't let oil get hot enough to smoke, and add more as needed.

Line a platter with paper towels and place it in the oven at 200 degrees. Pop each done cake into the oven to stay warm. Serve hot, topped with sour cream and green onions. A side dish of smoked salmon is great with latkes. Or go the sweet route, with berry preserves. After you master the traditional potato pancake, vary it by substituting mushrooms or grated zucchini for some of the potatoes and enriching with some Parmesan cheese. Add grated carrot for color, or grated orange peel zest for taste.

KUGELIS POTATO PANCAKES

The Lithuanians call these Kugelis, or bulviu plokstainis. Thanks go to Irena Blekys. Oven at 400F

4 medium potatoes, peeled and grated
1/2 onion, diced
2 slices bacon
1/4 cup milk
2 eggs, beaten
1 tsp salt
1/4 tsp pepper
1 TB flour

Put grated potatoes in a large mixing bowl. In an ovenproof skillet, fry cut-up bacon until crisp. Add bacon and most of its fat to the grated potatoes, then milk. Add eggs and mix well. Add salt, pepper and flour then mix again.

Scrape loose the remnants of frying the bacon. Pour the potato mixture into the greasy bacon skillet to pick up flavors.

Bake at 400F for 15 minutes. Reduce oven to 375F and bake 45 minutes until top is golden. Cut wedges. Serve with sour cream.

ZARELA'S POTATO FRITTERS

These are from Zarela Martinez' popular restaurant in Oaxaca, (wa HA ka) Mexico.

2 large potatoes
1 cup (1/4 pound) crumbled feta
2 large eggs, beaten
Salt and pepper to taste
Oil for frying

Peel and chop potatoes then boil until tender. Drain them, then mash with eggs, cheese, salt and pepper. Form into cakes about 1/2 inch thick and 3 or 4 inches in diameter and put these in the refrigerator 30 minutes, until they are firm. Heat oil in a fry pan, and slide the cakes in to sizzle until they begin to brown. Flip over and brown the other side. Keep in a warm oven until served. For variety, add 1/4 cup minced parsley, or 1/2 cup diced bell peppers or green onions to the mix

GOBI ALOO

In North India, this potato and cauliflower dish is a favorite.

3 cups thin sliced potato
1 medium head cauliflower, cut small
1/2 cup oil for frying
1/2 tsp each: black pepper, ginger powder, tumeric, cumin
1 cup yogurt
Salt and hot pepper to taste

In the oil, fry first the potatoes, then the cauliflower, until lightly browned. Add spices to the oil, then add them to the yogurt, salt and pepper. Toss with the veggies. Serve hot.

POTATO LAMB STEW

Savory and rich with herbs, this dish is popular in Spain. Or use beef, pork, or venison instead of lamb.

2 chopped onions
2 chopped bell peppers
1/4 cup olive oil
1-1/2 pounds lamb, cubed
3 cups water or stock
8 medium potatoes, peeled and quartered
4 cloves garlic
2 TB vinegar
3 TB cup minced parsley
1 TB each: paprika, dry thyme
3 bay leaves
Salt and pepper to taste
2 TB flour

Sauté the onion and peppers in the oil. Remove them and, in the same oil, sear the lamb cubes until the meat browns. Add water or stock, then garlic, parsley, paprika, bay leaves, vinegar, salt and pepper.

Cover and simmer 30 minutes. Add potatoes and simmer until they are soft. At the end, dissolve the flour in a little cool water and mix in this paste, to thicken the stew. Serve hot with a big salad.

Oven Baked Potato Dishes

PERFECT BAKED POTATOES

Russets are the starchiest of our potatoes. For crisp skins and flaky flesh, use russets, all about the same size so they cook in the same time. Scrub them well, then poke them a few times with a fork so steam can escape, and they won't burst.

If you wrap them in foil, they will be soggy. If you oil them, the skin will be soft, which is great if you like to eat nourishing potato skins. Preheat the oven to 425F, and set potatoes directly on the oven rack, not on a pan, and near the center of the oven. A medium potato will be done in just under an hour. For a quick lunch, microwave a medium potato about six minutes.

BUTTERMILK SCALLOPED POTATOES

Potatoes, cooked with milk or cheese, make a combination provide our bodies complete proteins, from the amino acids in both partners. If you have no buttermilk, use plain yogurt or one cup of milk mixed with a teaspoon of vinegar. Add various foods between layers of potatoes, such as onions, garlic-sauted greens or tasty smoked fish. Oven at 350F

3 cups potatoes, thin sliced
3 TB olive oil
3 TB flour
1 cup buttermilk
1 tsp salt
1/2 tsp mustard powder
1/4 tsp each: paprika, nutmeg

Trim and scrub potatoes. No need to peel. In a large bowl, toss the potato slices with the olive oil to coat them. Then toss with the flour. Lay them in a buttered casserole dish, layered with any enhancements. Mix the milk with salt and spices, and pour it over the potatoes. Bake one hour, or until potatoes are soft.

QUICK POTATOES GRATIN

This dish comes from an ancient Julia Child video made for black and white TV. Julia was young and thin and rather unsure of herself, but as funny ever. Like the above dish, it's basically potatoes cooked in milk. Oven at 450F

Start with a glass pie pan, or 8x8-inch baking dish. Fill it 1/2 full of thin sliced potatoes well washed in cold water to remove excess starch.

Heat two cups of milk and pour over the potatoes. Add a minced clove of garlic and 4 TB of butter on top. Then sprinkle with salt and pepper. Bake 25 minutes. Transform this dish into a meal by making it in a larger container and adding a layer of onions and of sliced Kielbasa or similar sausage. Add two beaten eggs to the milk, and, Voila! It's morphed into crust-less potato quiche. Know anyone gluten intolerant? No gluten here.

COLCANNON

Scottish potatoes with cabbage is a tasty dish with lots of protein, and perfect for a dark and stormy night.

3 cups yesterday's mashed potatoes
3 cups chopped cabbage
1 small onion, minced
1/2 cup milk
4 TB butter
Salt and pepper to taste
    Optional garnish: Grated cheese melted on top

Put mashed potatoes in a casserole. Steam cabbage until it wilts and add. Put onions in the milk and warm to almost boiling. Add butter to milk and let it melt. Mix into the potatoes and cabbage. Bake 20 minutes

TWICE BAKED POTATOES

Prepare these in advance, ready for the second baking. Mix in bits of crisp baco chips to add flavor. At our house, these are always a big hit. Oven at 400F

4 medium-large russet potatoes
1/2 cup grated cheese
1/2 stick butter
1/2 cup plain yogurt or sour cream
1 tsp each: thyme, minced garlic, tarragon
Salt and pepper to taste

Scrub potatoes, poke with a fork several times so steam can escape, then bake them one hour. Remove from the oven and, with mitts on, cut each potato in half, the long way, so they look like canoes. With a spoon, remove the white parts. In a large bowl, mix potato with the other ingredients. Refill potatoes, heaping up extra filling. Return them to the oven and bake 20 minutes more.

SEAFOOD STUFFED POTATOES

Prepare potatoes as for twice baked, above. Leave out the yogurt or sour cream and add one or two cups of cooked crab, scallops, clams or shrimp, smoked salmon or other smoked fish. Refill shells and bake 20 minutes.

ENGLISH SHEPHERD'S PIE

Popular pub fare in Britain, this is a great way to enjoy leftover mashed potatoes. Oven at 350F

Bottom layer:
2 cups cooked mashed potatoes
Filling:
1 cup chopped fresh or frozen vegetables
1 cup leftover chicken or other meat
Salt and pepper to taste
1/2 cup plain yogurt or sour cream
Optional: grated cheeses
Biscuit batter for crust:
1 cup flour
1 tsp baking powder
2 TB canola oil
1/4 tsp salt
1/2 tsp each: dry thyme, rosemary, parsley
1/3 cup milk

Layer mashed potatoes in the bottom of a baking dish. Add vegetables and meat, then a layer of yogurt or sour cream.

Mix biscuit crust ingredients, adding milk slowly as dough forms, or more flour or liquid as needed. Shape the dough with your hands and lay it on top of the pie. Bake the pie 45 minutes, or until the top is golden.

VEGGIE SIDE DISHES

A variety of interesting dishes made from local or home grown vegetables adds interest and nutrition to anyone's cooking repertoire. An old friend reminded me that most families have only a couple of dozen recipes they enjoy over and over. Maybe a few of these will make your list.

Spring Vegetables

SPRING MUSHROOMS AND SPINACH

Oven at 350F

4 cups chopped fresh mushrooms
1 cup chopped green onions
1/4 cup olive oil
Salt and pepper to taste
1/4 dry white wine
2 cups packed fresh spinach
1/4 cup grated Parmesan

In an ovenproof pan, toss mushrooms, salt and pepper in oil. Bake uncovered 30 minutes. Meanwhile, in a large fry pan, sauté onions over low to medium heat, in oil with salt and pepper until onions caramelize, nice and brown but not burned. This can be a tedious process. Add a little water to prevent burning.

Add wine and stir up the flavors stuck to the bottom of the pan. Add spinach and toss as it wilts. Remove cooked mushrooms from the oven and mix in the spinach and onions. Top with Parmesan cheese and bake another ten minutes.

SUPERB SPINACH

Steam spinach until it barely wilts. Let it cool, then use your hands to squeeze out most of the water. Return it to the pot and stir in butter and cream, a little salt and pepper. Re-warm and serve hot.

Optional garnish: minced green onions. Spinach is also tasty with lemon juice and olive oil with a little fresh marjoram and minced garlic. My childhood favorite was spinach with home made mayonnaise. Another great way to enjoy spinach is to mince some garlic, fry it a short time in olive oil, then add the spinach. Turn it a few times, until it wilts, then serve it hot.

BRAISED LEEKS

This is a simplified version of a leek dish served at Portland's Wildwood Restaurant. Oven at 350F

12 baby leeks, or 6 medium leeks
1/2 cup each: white wine, olive oil
4 sprigs thyme
4 ribs celery, thin sliced
1 small onion, thin sliced
2 TB capers, optional
4 cups baby greens
2 hard boiled eggs, peeled
Salt and pepper to taste

Clean leeks carefully, as they often have dirt between layers. If you use medium leeks, quarter them the long way. Lay leeks in a cast iron or other oven proof fry pan. Add wine, vinegar, oil and thyme. Heat until liquid starts to boil.

Place the pan in the oven for 10 minutes. Remove to add celery, onion and capers. Return to oven for 10 minutes.

Remove from oven and let pan cool. Then transfer contents to a covered dish and chill at least two hours, or overnight.

To serve, place leeks on each dish. Toss baby greens with veggies from the pan and their juices. Place a scoop of greens on top of each serving of leeks. Garnish with chopped hard cooked eggs, salt and pepper.

GREEK SAUTED SPRING GREENS

Greeks call it *spaniki mestafithes kai kou koonaria*. Don't try to say it, just whip it together and enjoy. The greens can include spinach (traditional), chard, kale, and others.

3 cups packed greens
1 chopped onion
1/4 cup olive oil
1/2 cup golden raisins
1/2 cup sunflower seeds
Salt and pepper to taste
1/4 cup lemon juice

In a large pot, sauté onion in oil until it's soft. Add greens, turning them as they cook down. Add raisins, sunflower seeds, salt and pepper. Serve at once, lemon juice squeezed over the top.

A tasty dish from Crete called *Horta Me Skortho* starts with the same greens, drops the raisins and seeds, but adds garlic, red pepper flakes and a topping of crumbled goats milk feta cheese.

GREEN BEANS WITH WALNUT SAUCE

This dish, with the yummy sauce, is served chilled in Istanbul. But some like it hot.

    Vegetables:
1 pound trimmed whole green beans
4 medium tomatoes, chopped
1 small onion, thin sliced
5 cloves garlic, minced
1/4 cup olive oil
1 tsp salt
    Walnut sauce:
1 cup chopped walnuts
1 cup small chunks of dry bread
3/4 cup milk
1 TB olive oil
Salt and pepper to taste

To make the sauce originally created by the Ottomans, whirl ingredients in a blender, adding milk as needed to form a thick but runny liquid. Set aside.

In a fry pan over medium heat, sauté onions and garlic in oil, with salt. Add green beans and tomatoes to the fry pan, cover and simmer 10 minutes. Drain off excess liquid. Chill or serve hot, in bowls with walnut sauce.

ASPARAGUS WITH PARMESAN
Oven at 400F

1 pound asparagus, thick is OK
2 TB olive oil
2 TB wine vinegar
    Garnish: 1/4 cup fresh grated Parmesan cheese
Salt and pepper to taste

Lay asparagus on a cookie sheet and brush with olive oil and vinegar. Bake 10 minutes then garnish and serve.

ASPARAGUS WITH GOAT CHEESE

Choose young slim spears and trim them. Salt some water in a fry pan and bring it to a boil. Slip in the spears. Return water to a boil and cook one minute. Lift spears into cold water to stop the cooking. Drain them and arrange on plates. Top with vinaigrette dressing, chopped sorrel, dollops of goat cheese, salt and pepper.

Summer Vegetable Sides

GREEN BEANS WITH CHERRIES

In early July, the first green beans are ready, and cherries are ripe. That's the time to enjoy them together in this dish from the gardens of Brittany.

1 pound young green beans
3 TB butter
1 cup pitted cherries
1 TB minced fresh tarragon
2 cloves minced garlic
2 TB minced parsley
Salt and pepper to taste

Trim the ends and cut beans into small pieces, on the diagonal. In a fry pan, melt the butter and stir in the beans, coating them. Add two tablespoons of water, cover and cook over low heat ten minutes. Add the cherries, herbs, salt and pepper. Heat and mix until the cherries are hot, then serve.

SUMMER SQUASH SAUTE

In August or September, choose one very fresh zucchini, one yellow crook neck and one patty pan summer squash, all medium sized. Slice them thin. Sauté quickly in a mix of half olive oil and half melted butter. Serve hot with sprigs of fresh marjoram, rosemary and thyme and salt to taste. Great with barbecued meat or fish.

SUWAT BEY'S ZUCCHINI

Suwat Bey was a noble Egyptian with a French wife. They served this simple dish one hot day beside the sea and close upon an ancient temple, in a town called Side (SEE deh) on the south coast of Turkey.

4 medium zucchinis
1/3 cup olive oil
3 TB balsamic vinegar
Salt and pepper to taste

Wash, trim ends and split each squash in half the long way. Lay them side by side in a large fry pan, add a little water and steam them until barely cooked. Place them whole, very carefully, in a flat, shallow dish one layer deep. Mix other ingredients and pour over.

Allow zucchini to marinate in the refrigerator at least two hours. Serve cold with stuffed eggs and bread and butter.

REAL RATATOUILLE   (Ra ta TU ee)

For a down home country favorite from the south of France, from mid-summer through fall, find these ingredients in the garden or at the farmers' market.
Oven at 350F

3 medium zucchini, sliced
1 medium eggplant, cut into 1/2" cubes
1 large red or yellow onion, thin sliced
2 green bell peppers, seeded and cut in thin strips
2 cups chopped ripe tomatoes
2 cloves garlic, crushed and minced
5 TB parsley, minced and set aside

Salt and pepper
1/3 cup olive oil

To remove bitter tastes, place cut-up zucchini and eggplant in two separate glass or ceramic bowls. Sprinkle each liberally with salt. Let them sit 30 minutes. Remove "sweat" droplets drying them with a dishtowel or paper towel.

In a heavy fry pan, sauté first zucchini then eggplant in olive oil until they start to brown. Next sauté the onions and peppers together. To them, add salt, pepper, tomatoes and garlic. Simmer until tomatoes are soft. Layer the vegetables into a heavy casserole pan, starting with one third of the tomato mixture, then one third of eggplant, then one third of zucchini, and top with one third of the parsley. Repeat twice. Bake 30 minutes.

SPICY CORN

Fresh corn, cut off the cob in summer or early fall is ideal. But canned or frozen corn will do in a pinch. You can even used canned tomatoes in winter.

2 cups cooked corn kernels
2 medium tomatoes, chopped
1/2 bell pepper, chopped
1 small onion, chopped
2 cloves garlic, minced
1 jalapeno chili, minced (or cayenne pepper to taste)
2 TB hulled sunflower seeds
3 TB olive oil
1 tsp each: dry mustard, cumin, paprika, coriander, turmeric
1/4 cup minced fresh parsley

Combine corn and tomatoes in a mixing bowl. In a large fry pan, saute bell pepper, onion, garlic, hot pepper and sunflower seeds in oil. Stir in the spices. Add the corn mix and simmer ten minutes. Remove from heat and add the parsley. Serve hot.

Or chill and serve the next day on a bed of young greens, as a salad.

STUFFED MUSHROOM CAPS

If you have ratatouille left over, strain out solids to use to stuff mushroom caps. Lay caps, top down and filling up, in a baking dish. Sprinkle on grated cheese. Bake 40 minutes at 350F.

SAVING RIPE TOMATOES

Diana Rattray, at her southern cooking website, says, "If you have an abundance of good fresh tomatoes, freeze them whole. Just wash, dry, and put them in freezer bags. They'll retain their flavor, and once thawed the peel will slip off easily. Use them in any recipes calling for fresh tomatoes except salads."

She also offers a number of unusual ways to use green tomatoes, including Fried Green Tomatoes, green tomato pie, and in relish or chutney.

TURKISH GREEN TOMATOES

In Turkey, green tomatoes appear often as a tasty, tart vegetable dish.

1 cup chopped onions
1/4 cup olive oil
3 cups chopped green tomatoes
1/2 cup stock
3 cloves minced garlic
Salt and pepper to taste
    Garnish: 1 cup crumbled feta cheese and 2 TB fresh dill weed

Sauté onions in oil until soft. Add tomatoes, stock, garlic, salt and pepper. Cover and simmer 15 minutes. Turks serve this dish on a platter, at room temperature, with garnish.

Fine Fall Vegetable Dishes

TARANTELLA CAULIFLOWER

1 medium head cauliflower
1/4 cup olive oil
1/4 cup chopped parsley
1/4 cup salt cured anchovies
Salt and hot chili flakes to taste
Chopped olives, optional

Remove center stem and slice the rest of the cauliflower into 1/4 inch thick slabs. Sauté these in the oil until soft. Add all the other ingredients and mix well. Add a little water, cover and simmer 20 minutes.

ITALIAN SAUTED VEGETABLES

Good fall veggie candidates include carrots, cauliflower, broccoli, parsnips, potatoes, kohlrabi, etc. Slice them thin and steam until barely cooked. Chop some onions, garlic and/or shallots. In a mix of butter and olive oil, sauté them along with pre-steamed vegetables in a big fry pan, with salt and pepper and a few nuts or seeds. Serve hot.

HOT PINK BEETS

The Maharaja of Mahmudabad served this bright pink beet dish to food author Madhur Jaffrey, near Lucknow, in India. There it's called chukandar dahi. Start with fresh or canned, sliced beets.

1 large or 2 medium beets
2 cups plain yogurt
3 TB minced fresh mint
3 cloves garlic, minced
2 TB oil
Salt, pepper and cayenne to taste

Boil whole clean beets until tender, then cool them and rub off peel. Slice them. Sauté garlic in oil, then add garlic and oil to the yogurt. Add mint, salt and peppers and mix vigorously. Add flavored yogurt to sliced beets and stir gently.

BUTTERNUT SQUASH CHEZ PANISSE

In keeping with Alice Waters' highest standards, select the freshest finest ingredients for the best outcome.

2 pounds butternut or any winter squash
1/4 cup lime juice
Fresh cilantro
Salt to taste

Bake or microwave the squash until the meat is soft. Cut open and separate meat from peel. Mash meat with lime juice and salt. Place in a serving dish and scatter cilantro leaves over it. Serve hot.

HONEY CARROTS

Good as they are raw, surprisingly carrots are more nutritious cooked with a little fat. And it's true they are good for the eyesight, high in Vitamin A and other carotenoids, which also inhibit tumors and stimulate the immune system. For carrots everyone will love, buy organic, looking lively with the tops still on. Wash but don't peel them.

1 pound fresh organic carrots
1 TB butter
1 TB honey
1 tsp lemon juice
1/2 tsp salt
Dash of cayenne pepper

Clean and chop carrots. Simmer 8 minutes or until soft. In a medium pan, melt butter and add honey, lemon and salt. Drain carrots (save the juice for stock) and add to the butter pan, then stir well to coat all of them. Serve hot with a sprinkle of paprika on top.

CARROTS MOROCCAN STYLE

4 medium-large carrots
1/2 tsp salt
4 cloves garlic, minced
1/4 cup red wine vinegar
1/2 tsp each cumin and coriander
Cayenne pepper to taste

Clean carrots and slice them into thin disks. In water with salt and garlic, simmer carrots about 10 minutes. Drain off the liquid and save for stock.

Mix cumin, coriander and cayenne into the vinegar and pour it over the carrots. Serve hot.

PUMPKIN CARROT MASH

1 pound cooked pumpkin meat, chunked
1 pound carrots, trimmed and chopped
2 TB each: olive oil, butter, honey or sugar
1/2 tsp each: nutmeg, cinnamon, cayenne
Salt and pepper to taste

Steam carrots until soft. Combine with cooked pumpkin. Add remaining ingredients and mash. Serve hot

RED CABBAGE SUPREME

Cabbage is high in indoles, which modulate estrogen metabolism and may be why women in Eastern Europe, where everyone eats lots of cabbage, have lower rates of breast cancer than women in the west. Red cabbage also has lots of anthocyanins, powerful antioxidant flavinoids.

1/2 medium red (purple) cabbage
1 medium red onion, sliced thin
2 tart apples, cored and chopped
2 TB caraway seeds
3 TB canola oil
Salt and pepper to taste

Shred the cabbage then saute it with the onion in oil until both are wilted. Add apples, caraway, salt and pepper. Cover and remove from heat. Let stand ten minutes to barely cook apples. Serve hot.

CRISPY PARSNIP CHIPS

These are easy to make and a special treat. Scrub parsnips, peel them and slice thin. Or use the vegetable peeler to make long curls. Drop pieces into hot olive oil (350F). They will cook very quickly. Drain them on paper towel, sprinkle with salt and serve with chicken or other main dish.

Experiment using other root vegetables, curls or thin slices. Never fry in oil that got hot enough to smoke. When an oil or fat over-heats, the chemistry is changed and it will not only taste bad, but do your health no good. Olive oil, coconut oil, beef fat, clarified butter (ghee) and lard all do well under high heat.

SAUSAGE AND CABBAGE (Saucisse aux chou)
Oven at 350F

1 pound spicy pork sausage
1 medium head of cabbage, shredded
1/4 tsp each: salt, nutmeg, black pepper, dry thyme and parsley
1 bay leaf
1 cup stock
1 TB cornstarch

Fry the sausage until nearly done. Into a large pot, put two chunks of sausage, salt, nutmeg, pepper, thyme, parsley and bay plus the stock. Add the cabbage and simmer for ten minutes.

Using tongs, lift half the cooked cabbage into a casserole, then add all the sausage, then the remaining cabbage. Mix the cornstarch with a little water to form a paste and mix this into the stock left in the pot. Pour this over the cabbage. Bake 20 minutes.

BEETS, CABBAGE AND CRANBERRIES

3 TB olive oil
1-1/2 cup shredded red (purple) cabbage
1-1/2 cup cooked beets, diced
1 cup fresh cranberries
2 TB honey
1/4 tsp each: ginger, allspice
Salt and pepper to taste

In a large pot, sauté the cabbage in oil about five minutes. Add the beets and all other ingredients. Cover and simmer about 8 minutes. Serve hot.

TUSCAN FENNEL

Oven at 400F

2 fennel bulbs, sliced thin
1/2 onion, chopped
2 cloves garlic, minced
3 TB olive oil
2 cups chopped fresh or canned tomatoes
1 tsp each: dry rosemary and thyme, sugar
1/2 tsp nutmeg
Salt and pepper to taste
1 cup breadcrumbs
1/2 cup grated Parmesan or Romano cheese

Sauté fennel, onion and garlic in olive oil until onions are soft. Add tomatoes, herbs, nutmeg, salt and pepper. Cover and simmer five minutes. Transfer to an ovenproof dish and top with breadcrumbs and grated hard cheese. Bake 20 minutes or until the top begins to brown.

FENNEL WITH BUTTER AND GARLIC

Fennel is delicate and tasty, and easy prepare and to grow, all reasons why it is becoming better known.

2 medium fennel bulbs, and stems
2 cloves garlic, minced
3 TB butter, melted
1/2 tsp salt
1/4 tsp nutmeg
2 tsp flour

Trim fennel bulbs and cut up. Melt butter and sauté garlic. Add fennel slices, salt and nutmeg and stir. Add 1/2 cup water. Simmer about 15 minutes. Mix flour with a little water, then stir this mix into the liquid until it thickens.

GOURMET CABBAGE AND SPINACH

Eating cabbage and kraut we benefit from the mopping up of free radicals (not the political kind), as well as from the fiber and high levels of calcium, magnesium, potassium and Vitamin K in cabbage and spinach.

1/4 cup roasted, salted sunflower seeds
1/2 large fresh cabbage, thin sliced
1 large bundle of fresh spinach, cleaned, stems removed
3 TB olive oil
2 TB balsamic vinegar
2 cloves garlic, minced
1 tsp each: honey, Dijon mustard
Salt to taste

Thin slice the cabbage, then clean the spinach and remove most of the stems. In a large fry pan, sauté sunflower seeds in oil. Add cabbage and toss, then cover and cook over low heat until it wilts (about 8 minutes).

While cabbage cooks, whisk together balsamic, garlic, honey, Dijon and salt to make a dressing. Over low heat, add spinach to cabbage, then the dressing. Turn mixture until spinach just wilts. Serve at once. Delicious with ham.

Veggie Sides in Winter

CURRIED CARROTS AND PARSNIPS
Oven at 350F

7 carrots, sliced
2 parsnips, peeled and sliced
1 large onion, in peeled chunks
2 TB curry powder
1 cup orange marmalade
1/2 cup cream

Combine and mix ingredients in a casserole. Cover and bake 40 minutes or until veggies are soft. If you have no marmelade, substitute a finely chopped fresh orange with about half its peel, plus 1/3 cup honey.

BROCCOLI FRITTERS

In Brittany, people dip small vegetable fritters in flavored mayonnaise or serve them with seafood. Try them also made with cauliflower, instead of broccoli.

   Batter:
1 cup flour
2 eggs, beaten
1 cup milk
1/2 tsp each: salt, pepper, thyme
   Vegetables:
1 cup broccoli florettes, chopped small
3 TB cider vinegar
2 TB minced parsley
Salt and pepper to taste
Oil for frying

Steam the broccoli five minutes, then chill in cold water to stop the cooking. Marinade the cooked broccoli, sprinkled with vinegar, parsley, salt and pepper for one half hour, at room temperature. Heat oil in a fry pan.

Lift some broccoli and with the same large spoon, pick up some batter. Drop them together in the oil to form a small flat fritter. Fry until both sides are golden and serve hot.

HEAVEN AND EARTH (Himmel und Erd)

This German winter dish refers to apples growing up high and potatoes and turnips growing down underground. Similar recipes combine turnips and potatoes, both plentiful in winter, some with cheese. Or use pear instead of apple.

1 large potato
1 large turnip
1 large apple
1/2 tsp each: salt, pepper, mustard powder
2 TB honey
2 TB lemon juice, or cider vinegar
3 TB butter or more if desired

Clean, trim and cut up potato, turnip and apple. Simmer in salted water until they are soft, about 20 minutes. Add pepper, honey, lemon juice or vinegar, and mustard then mash with the butter as it melts. Serve hot.

RUTABABA DELIGHT

Choose small roots, no more than three inches across.

3 medium rutabagas
1 cup mixed dry fruits
1/2 cup red wine
2 TB butter
3 TB dry chives
1 tsp dried thyme
Salt and pepper to taste

Peel and slice rutabagas, then steam or simmer them until tender. Meanwhile, soak dry fruit in the wine. When the rutabagas are cooked, drain them and put them in a fry pan with butter, chives and thyme. Saute until they start to brown. Then add wine and fruit mix and salt and pepper.

Cover and simmer over low heat about five minutes. Good with a roast or meat stew.

BEETS, GREENS AND 'SHROOMS

For greens, use kale, chard, mustard, beet tops, bak choi, collards, or others. Oven at 350F

3 medium golden or white beets
3 cups packed greens
2 cups wild or white mushrooms
1/2 stick butter
1/2 cup thin sliced onion
1/4 cup stock
3 TB vinegar
Salt and pepper to taste

Scrub and trim beets, oil them and wrap in foil. Bake one hour. While beets roast, clean greens then slice them into two-inch lengths.

Melt the butter and brown it until it smells nutty, then add the onions and mushrooms. Sauté them about four minutes then add the greens, stirring as they wilt. Add stock, salt and pepper, then cover the pan and simmer ten minutes.

Cool the roasted beets, peel, slice and toss them with vinegar. Transfer greens and mushrooms into a large serving dish and place beets on top. Serve hot.

CREAMED SWISS CHARD

Chard is hardy enough that it will grow through most of our winters, west of the mountains. Harvest all you can use when temperatures below 20 are predicted as a hard frost will damage plants. Plants get tough with heavy rain beating on them. Use the thin part of the leaves in this recipe.

About twelve large chard leaves
2 TB butter
1 onion, chopped
1/2 cup grated cheese
1/2 cup cream
1/4 tsp nutmeg
Salt and pepper to taste
1 egg, beaten

Use only the green part of the chard leaves, saving stems for stock or vegetable soup. Steam until they are tender, longer if they are tougher. Chill leaves in cold water. Squeeze out the water, and chop cooked chard.

Melt butter in a fry pan and sauté the onion about three minutes. Add chard, cheese, cream, nutmeg, salt and pepper. Heat and stir to mix. When the mix is hot, turn off the heat and pour in the egg. Cover and let egg cook in residual heat.

CHARD STEMS

The stems are so much sturdier than the leaves that you can treat them as a different vegetable. If you grow chard, you'll have more than enough.

Chop stems into one-inch pieces and simmer in salted water until they are tender. Add them to a casserole, to meat sauce for pasta, or use with pizza topping. Put them in quiche. Make them the basis for a small casserole with tomatoes, fresh herbs and top with cream and grated cheese. Thanks, Alice Waters, for the great ideas.

CAVOLINI ALLA ROMANA

(Little Brussels sprouts, Roman style)
Choose small sprouts. Mince some garlic. Saute sprouts and garlic in olive oil until sprouts soften. Add chopped ham or prosciutto. Serve hot.

WINTER WHITE VEGGIE PUREE

3 medium white potatoes
1 large turnip
1 white onion
1 celery root (celeriac)
6 cloves garlic
1/2 stick butter
1/4 cup sour cream or plain yogurt
Salt and pepper to taste

Peel and chop all the vegetables, then steam them with garlic until they are soft. Drain off the liquid and transfer vegetables to a food processor. Puree with butter, sour cream, salt and pepper. Serve hot.

PARSNIP AND POTATO PUREE

Alice Waters again... Peel and dice two cups each of potatoes and parsnips. Cook separately, in salted water until each is tender. Combine and puree. Add salt and pepper, cream and butter until they are just right.

ABOUT OVEN ROASTED VEGETABLES

Dry heat and an uncovered pan, brings out the sweetness and unique flavors of root vegetables. Try small potatoes, carrots, parsnips, beets, turnips, rutabagas, Brussels sprouts and winter squash. Have all pieces about the same size pieces so they cook in nearly the same time. Toss with oil and a little salt, some fresh or dry herbs and put them in a baking pan. Bake at 400F for 45 to 60 minutes, depending on size of chunks. Overcook and the result is hard and dry.

ROASTED WINTER ROOTS
Oven at 450F

2 cups potatoes, cubed
2 cups winter squash, peeled and cubed
8 cloves garlic, minced
2 medium onions, chunked
2 tsp minced fresh sage
3 TB maple syrup
3 TB olive oil
Salt and pepper to taste

Toss all ingredients in a large bowl. Spread them in a single layer in a large casserole or ovenproof fry pan. Cover and roast 40 minutes, uncovering to stir every 10 minutes. Serve hot.

ITALIAN ROASTED WINTER VEGGIES

Use carrots, potatoes, winter squash, rutabagas, turnips, kohlrabi, broccoli, shallots or onions. Clean and cut all to similar sized chunks. In a large bowl, toss them with olive oil, fresh rosemary and salt. Place veggies in a baking pan, add one quarter cup of water and cover pan with foil. Roast at 425F. After fifteen minutes, add whole mushrooms if desired. Cook until a fork goes into the potatoes easily

BREAKFAST AND BRUNCH

For special mornings, or when family or friends stay with you, a good breakfast plan makes things simpler. My favorite breakfast for such occasions is a big fruit salad and some sort of egg and potato casserole that I can make in advance and just pop in the oven, and later keep warm for those who sleep in.

A few ideas help make a morning meal for family and friends. Pancakes, waffles, quick fruit and nut bread, coffee cake, fruit salad, quiche, muffins, bread pudding, breakfast burrito, bagels and cream cheese with lox, crepes filled with ricotta and fruit, English muffins topped with mashed avocado and a slice of tomato, potato pancakes with applesauce, French toast, croissants with marmalade, toast with peanut butter, granola with yogurt and fruit, oatmeal with a side of bacon, rewarmed pizza, quick frying pan quesadillas.

BISCUITS WITH MUSHROOM GRAVY
Oven at 350F

    Biscuits:
2 cups flour
1 tsp baking powder
1 tsp thyme
1/2 tsp salt
1/3 cup canola oil
3/4 cup milk

Gravy:
1/2 pound pork sausage or cut up links
1/2 pound sliced mushrooms
1/4 cup diced onion
3 TB oil
4 TB flour
2 cups milk
1 tsp dark soy sauce
Salt and pepper to taste

Mix up biscuit ingredients and with floured hands form eight round mounds. Bake about 13 minutes or until the tops are light brown.

For gravy, sauté sausage, mushrooms and onion in oil. Add flour and mix well with the fat. Slowly add milk as it thickens. Add soy sauce for flavor and color, then salt and pepper. Serve hot over fresh biscuits.

BERRY FINE FRENCH TOAST

Al Johnson taught me to leave sliced bread out overnight, so it absorbs more egg dip and makes richer French Toast. Serve this as a special breakfast or in smaller servings as a dessert. You can use frozen berries, but warm them up a bit. Oven at 350F

   Batter dip:
8 slices of bread
5 eggs
2 cups milk
2 TB honey
1/2 tsp salt
1 tsp vanilla

Topping:
2 cups fresh berries
1 cup whole milk yogurt
1/4 cup honey or to taste
1/2 cup filberts, diced

Cut bread into cubes and arrange in a baking dish. Beat eggs with milk, honey, salt and vanilla. Pour this over the bread. Bake 30 minutes or until eggs are set.

Meanwhile mix remaining berries, milk and honey. When the baking is done, cut into squares. Drench each in plenty of topping and scatter nuts on top.

DAWN'S MORNING CASSEROLE

Dawn Presta ran a café in Yreka, then B&Bs on San Juan Island, and later cooked at a winery inn outside Walla Walla. She became adept at breakfasts for a group, making this casserole often. Oven at 350F

3 medium potatoes -- wash and slice thin
1/2 cup chopped bell pepper
1/2 cup chopped onion
8 eggs beaten
4 oz grated cheese
1 tsp thyme (or fresh basil)
1 tsp dill weed
2 TB olive oil

Oil a baking dish, then make a layer of potatoes on the bottom. Add peppers and onion, and pour in eggs. Sprinkle with grated cheese, and top that with a scattering of thyme and dill. Bake about 50 minutes or until eggs are set firmly.

ZUCCHINI OMELET

Did your two zucchini plants produce enough for a family of twelve? Good time to try this tasty baked omelet. Oven at 350F

8 eggs, beaten
1 medium zucchini, thin sliced or grated
1 small onion, chopped
3 TB olive oil
1/2 cup crumbled feta or similar cheese
Basil, thyme, salt and pepper to taste

In a large fry pan, saute onion and zucchini in oil, until onion is soft. Pour in beaten eggs. Stir them to allow them to cook on the bottom. After they cook for a minute, sprinkle in cheese, herbs, salt and pepper. Pop the pan into the hot oven. Bake 10 minutes or until eggs are set.

BAKED SPINACH OMELET
Oven at 350F

8 eggs
1/2 cup cream
2 cloves garlic, minced
2 chopped tomatoes
2 cups packed spinach
1/4 cup olive oil
Salt and pepper to taste

Beat eggs with cream then set aside. In a large fry pan, sauté garlic in oil. Add tomatoes, salt and pepper. Simmer five minutes, uncovered. Add spinach and turn it over as it wilts. Put this mix into a baking dish. Pour eggs on top. Stir to mix. Bake 25 minutes.

WHEAT BERRY PUDDING

When we lived in Central Oregon, we bought a 100-pound sack of wheat right off our farming neighbor's combine. The chickens ate some and I grew muscles grinding wheat by hand, for bread. Unprocessed wheat seeds take forever to cook. Start the night before and wake to find them done.

1/2 cup wheat berries
2 cups boiling water
1/2 tsp salt
2 cups fresh or frozen berries
1 cup chopped dried fruit or raisins
1 egg, beaten
2 cups milk
1/4 cup each: honey, toasted nuts
1/2 tsp each: vanilla, cinnamon, nutmeg

To cook the wheat berries, put them in a thermos and add salt and boiling water. In eight or ten hours, the water will be absorbed and the berries will be warm and soft. In a large bowl, mix cooked wheat with the other ingredients. Bake 30 minutes at 350F

SUMMER BERRY CREPES

Call these egg-y pancakes, crepes or blinzes, and enjoy them for breakfast or dessert with cottage cheese or ricotta and berry filling. If great flavor is not reason enough to eat blackberries, raspberries and their cousins, eat them for fiber, powerful antioxidants, bio-flavinoids, anti-allergens, several anti-cancer factors and natural sugars for energy, fresh or frozen.

    Crepes:
1/2 cup milk
2 beaten eggs
1/2 cup white flour
1/4 tsp salt
    Filling:
1 cup cottage cheese or ricotta
1/2 cup smashed blackberries
2 TB warm honey
1/2 tsp nutmeg
    Topping:
2 cups smashed berries
1/4 cup warm honey

Mix crepe ingredients. Pour batter into a lightly oiled fry pan and let it spread to form rounds six to eight inches across. Cook over medium heat, flipping to lightly brown second side. Keep them warm. When you have all of them made, put about 1/4 cup filling on each and roll them up. Pour topping over them and serve warm.

PUMPKIN PANCAKES

These pancake are a treat when you have overnight guests and want to serve them a special breakfast. To make these cakes super nutritious, add 1 TB flax seed meal and 2 TB of wheat germ.

1 cup pureed pumpkin
2 beaten eggs
2 cups flour
2 tsp baking powder + 1 TB baking soda
2 cups buttermilk
2 TB vegetable oil
1 Tsp each: salt, sugar, cinnamon, cloves, ginger, nutmeg

Mix all ingredients in a large bowl. Ladle batter onto a hot, oiled griddle or fry pan. When the top is bubbly, flip pancake over. Enjoy these with jam or lots of butter and maple syrup.

PEAR PANCAKES FOR FALL

This pancake is delicious for company breakfast, or for dessert with extra honey. Good with apples or berries too. Think of it as a fruit fritatta.

4 beaten eggs
1/4 cup honey
1 cup flour
1 tsp vanilla
Pinch of salt
1 cup milk
1 firm pear, cored and thin sliced
3/4cup dried fruit (apricots, raisins, cranberries, prunes)

Mix all except dry fruit, until batter is smooth. Add fruit and stir. Oil a fry pan. Turn on the broiler so it's ready for the next step. Pour batter in a hot pan. Cook over medium heat the bottom is light brown. Now, broil the top until its no longer liquid. Or you can leave it a moment longer to lightly brown.

CASUAL MEALS

Pizza from Scratch

BASIC YEAST DOUGH

This quantity makes a large pizza or two big calzones. For a pizza base, you can also use large wheat tortillas, pita bread or focaccia. We've made little pizza variants on crisp toast or on rounds of polenta. But a real crust calls for basic yeast dough. It's easy, once you learn how.

1 cup flour
1/2 cup warm water
1 tsp dry yeast
1 tsp sugar
1/4 tsp salt
1 tsp olive oil
extra flour for dusting

In the blender puree water, yeast, sugar and 1/2 cup flour, pushing down any uncooperative flour with a rubber spatula. Puree it again, for a total of about one minute. Now wait about 15 minutes while the warm water and sugar get the yeast growing well without any salt to slow them down. Dump the puree into a wide mixing bowl and stir in first the salt, then the remaining flour.

Dust a quarter cup of flour onto a clean, flat surface. Oil your clean hands and dig in, removing all the dough from the bowl and dropping the dough into the dusting of flour. Knead it, adding flour as required as it develops elasticity.

This won't take long because that blender action already developed much of the gluten into fibers. Knead until it feels smooth and fleshy - punch, press, roll, fold, punch, press, roll, fold. Five minutes is good.

Now put it in a warm place (130F is ideal) and leave it to double in size. The time for rising depends entirely on the temperature of the dough. At 130F it doubles in about 45 minutes. At room temperature, two hours is typical. When it has doubled, punch it down and reshape it. Roll it out to about 1/4 inch thickness. For pizza, work your dough until it's large and flat. Round is good, but square will taste the same. This dough will make two large or four small calzone.

It will puff again during the baking of pizza or calzone. For rolls or bread, shape it and let it rise again before shaping it for crust. Bake pizza at 425 F at home, calzone at 375F.

Originally, la signora used her leftovers to make pizza. But you can get creative, like the top chefs. Exact quantities are unimportant. Experiment. Do you prefer your crust thin or thick, your sauce plentiful, or your cheese well browned? Make your own and have it your way. Bake your pizza in a hot, hot oven until it's sizzling and the crust is starting to brown, ten to fifteen minutes. You can make a large batch of dough, divide it up and freeze it. To thaw, leave it out from morning until dinner time.

HOME MADE TOMATO SAUCE

Marcella Hazan's perfectly simple sauce makes a good base for pizza toppings. Start with 5 medium-large tomatoes. Hold each in boiling water about 30 seconds to scald the skin, then cool it. The skin will slide off easily. Now quarter the slippery things and remove seeds and juice. Chop them up and put them in a saucepan. Add a whole peeled onion.

Simmer, without a cover, about 45 minutes. Remove the onion. Add 4 TB butter and smash the tomatoes. Add salt and pepper as needed. You'll get pretty good results with canned or frozen tomatoes.

Pizza Topping Ideas

SUMMER SQUASH PIZZA
Cover the crust with a layer of prepared tomato sauce. Add thin slices of zucchini or other summer squash. Scatter lots of goat cheese morsels and minced fresh sage.

PIZZA LUCHESE
Start with a thin layer of mozzarella on the crust. Scatter prosciutto ham and chopped dry or fresh figs. Top with lots of Gorgonzola or blue cheese.

POTATO AND SMOKED SALMON PIZZA
Lay on thin potato slices mixed with a little whole milk plain yogurt. Add chunks of smoked salmon, a scattering of chopped celery and chopped green onions. Cover with grated mozzarella cheese.

WILD MUSHROOM PIZZA
Cover the crust with a layer of sliced mushrooms mixed with sour cream. Add sliced leeks, red or green pepper slices, fresh oregano and thyme. Sprinkle with Parmesan.

SAUSAGE AND VEGETABLE
Spread tomato sauce on the crust. Chop 2 cups of a mix of tomatoes, zucchini, celery, carrot and cabbage. Steam veggies until barely cooked, then spread evenly on the tomato sauce. Add small chunks of spicy pork sausage, (or tempeh to keep it veggie) minced onion, some fresh thyme and marjoram. Cover lightly with grated cheddar.

CORN AND RICOTTA PIZZA
Cover the crust with a layer of ricotta cheese mixed with grated Parmesan, pepper. Spread fresh, corn kernels, then chopped meat, minced garlic and a cup of mix of raw celery, tomatoes, cabbage and zucchini. Top with crumbled feta cheese.

HAM AND APPLE PIZZA
Spread the crust with Ragu sauce, scatter diced ham over the crust then thin apple slices and a little diced onion. Crumble bleu or Gorgonzola cheese over all.

SPINACH AND BLEU CHEESE PIZZA
Spread the crust with basil pesto sauce, then scatter chopped, barely steamed fresh spinach, sliced mushrooms and bleu cheese. Add some sliced fresh tomatoes and a thin layer of grated mozzarella. Thanks to Courtney and her mom Judy Smith for testing this one with a thin crust. It was a hit at a party.

ONION, WALNUT AND BLEU CHEESE PIZZA
Spread 3 tablespoons of olive oil on the crust. Thin slice one onion and scatter it over the oiled crust. Sprinkle on 1 cup walnuts, then 1 or 2 cups crumbled bleu cheese.

PIZZA ITALIANA
Spread a crust with bottled marinara sauce. Sauté two sliced onions in 2 TB butter until tender. Spread onion atop sauce. Add a cup chopped fresh cilantro or parsley, 1/2 cup grated provolone. Bake on the middle shelf of the oven for 11 minutes. Remove, add 1 cup chopped tomatoes and 1 cup crumbled feta cheese. Bake on the bottom shelf for two minutes more. Tested by Judy and Courtney Smith.

Pita Pocket Ideas

Cut off one edge to open the pocket, or slice across the middle for two half pockets. Make a sauce of plain yogurt spiced with garlic, paprika, cumin, coriander, salt and pepper. Drizzle on plenty of sauce after you fill the pocket with one of these tasty combinations:

Sliced lamb, thin sliced onion, chopped cucumber

Chicken chunks, crumbled feta, chopped tomatoes and chopped lettuce

Two or three falafels, fresh spinach leaves, chopped green onions

Cooked white beans or garbanzos, crumbled bacon, sorrel leaves

Tofu, chopped walnuts, leaf lettuce, chopped tomatoes, fresh basil leaves

Hummous and salad greens with mustard dressing.

Sandwich Ideas

Use all sorts of bread to make inspired sandwiches. Buy bread un-sliced and you can cut firm but thin slices for sandwiches. Too thick, and the sandwich tastes dry.

On dark bread try cheddar cheese, thin tart apple slices, mayonnaise

Into a whole-wheat pita, put tart apple slices and crunchy peanut butter.

On multi-grain bread spread tahini and fruit jam. Top with sliced bananas.

On hearty bread, melt some bleu cheese. Top with toasted walnuts and dry cranberries.

Mix some grated jack cheese, salsa and sour cream. Spread this on toast.

On Jewish rye bread, lay slices of leftover meat, some coleslaw or sauerkraut, top with creamy salad dressing.

Split a baguette the long way. Slather with Grey Poupon or other spicy mustard, lay in turkey or chicken slices, tart apple slices, thin sliced onion and/or arugula.

On toasted Italian bread, brush olive oil, then sprinkle parmesan and garlic powder, add sliced provolone or jack cheese, melt this in the broiler then top with roasted red pepper.

On any bread try tofu pate, sliced cucumbers, salt and pepper.

On an English muffin, spread cream cheese, and basil pesto sauce. Or mix cream cheese with canned tuna and use this as a spread. Good on crackers, too.

Spread a tortilla with pesto, hummus or bean mash. Fill with chopped fresh greens.

Spread a large tortilla with cream cheese. Add cropped fresh salad makings and some salsa. Roll up tight and cut into rounds. Serve as party food.

On a warm English muffin, pile leftover mushrooms, watercress or mustard greens.

Mix tuna with an equal volume of minced fresh greens. Spread on sourdough toast.

On hearty wheat bread, spread soft brie cheese and apricot jam.

On white toast, lay some turkey slices, cranberry sauce, lettuce, salt and pepper

On rye bread spread spicy mustard, add thin sliced meat and thin sliced pears.

On any bread, spread spicy mustard on one side, mayo on the other. Lay in sliced tofu and sliced fresh tomatoes.

FRUITS AND DESSERTS

Desserts made from locally grown fruit are delicious and healthful. Though these recipes call for fresh fruits, you can use canned or frozen in most of them.

Spring Fruit Treats

RHUBARB PUDDING

Growing rhubarb is easy. Start in winter with root crowns at least three feet apart, rather than seeds. By April, you've got your first small crop. Plants grow anew from roots each spring. The leaves are not eaten because they are loaded with irritating oxalic acid. Stems can be very tart, especially green stems, so add plenty of sugar or honey.   Oven at 350F

    Pudding:
3 cups chopped rhubarb stems
1/4 cup melted butter
2 eggs
3/4 cup white flour
1/2 cup sugar
1 tsp vanilla
1/4 tsp salt
1 cup milk or half-and-half
    Topping:
1/4 cup butter
3/4 cup brown sugar
3/4 cup cream

Melt butter and spread it in the bottom of a casserole. In a mixing bowl, combine remaining pudding ingredients. Pour into casserole.

Bake 40 minutes or until the edges start to brown. Serve hot, with a topping of hot butter mixed with brown sugar and chilled cream.

RHUBARB COMPOTE

As children, we loved a dish of tasty rhubarb from our grandmother's neglected garden, all sugared and warm, for breakfast, with eggs and grits. Make it well-sweetened, and enjoy the earliest of the fruity produce.

6 large fresh rhubarb stems, thin sliced
1/3 cup apple juice
1/3 cup sugar, or to taste
1 tsp cinnamon

Simmer rhubarb and apple juice on low heat 15 minutes or until rhubarb is soft. Add sugar and cinnamon. Stir well.

FRUIT CRISP

Rhubarb is ready in April or May and if well-watered will still be producing until the last freeze. Later in the year, make this dessert with cherries or other soft summer fruits, or fresh or frozen berries, or a combination. Vary amount of honey tartness of the fruit. Oven at 350F

    Filling:
6 cups chopped fruit
1/4 to 1/2 cup warm honey
3 TB melted butter
3 TB flour
1 tsp cinnamon

Topping:
1/2 cup flour
1 cup quick oat meal
2/3 cup brown sugar
1/2 cup melted butter

Mix fruit with honey, butter, flour and cinnamon. Flour thickens the juice. Spread into a buttered baking dish. Mix topping ingredients in a bowl. Using your hand, sprinkle evenly over fruit. Bake 45 to 50 minutes.

Summer Fruit Delights

CHERRY BERRY YUM

Cherries ripen in June and early July. The trees thrive all over our region. Pitted or not, cherries freeze well. As kids, we'd climb into the huge branches and pick from an ancient tree by an abandoned homestead in the San Juan Islands. This dessert can be made with any fruit or berry. Wild blackberries, at their peak in August, are superb.

2 cups fruit, small pieces
1 cup red wine
1 cup broken filbert meats
Pound cake or angel food cake

Soak fruit in wine overnight. Serve as a sauce over pound cake, with a scattering of nuts. Or, for a summer celebration, pick berries, add a little sweetener, and mash them. Serve cake slices drenched in berries with a dollop of delicious whipped cream on top.

STRAWBERRY SHORTCAKE

In our family, shortcake was a huge treat. Strawberries are at their best in June, but ever-bearing garden varieties produce much longer. If you can't wait for summer, make this dessert with frozen berries. For higher nutrients, substitute 1/4 cup wheat germ or oat bran for 1/4 cup of the flour. Oven at 375F

Biscuits:
2 cups flour
1/3 cup soft butter
1 TB brown sugar
2 tsp baking powder
1/4 tsp salt
2/3 cup milk, or rich cream (YUM!)
Berries:
3 cups strawberries, trimmed and sliced
1/2 cup sugar
Topping:
1 cup heavy cream, whipped
2 tsp powdered sugar

In a bowl, mix dry biscuit ingredients with a fork. Cut in butter and add milk or cream. With oiled hands, knead until dough holds together. Shape biscuits one-half inch thick and two to three inches across. Lay rounds on an oiled cookie sheet, well separated. Bake 20 minutes or until biscuits begin to brown.

While biscuits bake, mash berries with sugar, and whip the cream. When biscuits are done, cool then split them. On each plate, set half a biscuit, ladle on strawberries, add the other half of the biscuit and more strawberries. For the topping, beat fresh cream then stir in the sugar.

BERRY SIPPER

In summer, when berries are ripe, puree them with honey and add to lemonade or sparkling seltzer. In winter, use frozen berries to puree and add to fruit juices, hot tea, or yogurt milkshake smoothies. My favorite juice is a seedless blend of lemonade and wild blackberry juice. Make the juice by thawing frozen berries and using a coarse weave strainer to remove the seeds. It's superb in winter.

BUDAPEST CHERRY SOUP

Elegant cafes in Hungary serve this summer treat.

2 cups pitted cherries
1 cup water
1/2 cup sugar
1/2 stick cinnamon
1/8 tsp salt
1 TB cornstarch
1/2 cup red wine
1 TB lemon juice
1/2 cup sour cream
   Garnish: Cinnamon, Sour cream

Simmer cherries, water, sugar, stick cinnamon and salt or five minutes. Dissolve cornstarch in the wine and add this to the cherries, stirring as soup thickens. Remove 1/2 cup of soup and mix it with lemon juice and 1/4 cup sour cream, then return this to the pot. Mix well. Chill to serve, each bowl topped with a white dollop of sour cream and a sprinkle of powdered cinnamon.

BERRY PEACHY

This fresh fruit dessert depends on the sensuous lushness of perfect peaches at the height of summer.

3 medium peaches
1/2 cup honey, warm
1 cup white wine
1 cup raspberries
1 cup blueberries
Zest of one lemon
20 fresh mint leaves

Choose peaches that are just slightly soft, with a wonderful aroma. Wash and peel them, remove pits, then slice them about 1/2 inch thick. Put them in a large bowl and add honey and berries. Remove just the yellow oily part of the lemon peel in thin strips. Add that, and the mint leaves. Stir gently. Serve chilled.

SUMMER FRUIT AND NUT CAKE
Oven at 350F

1 cup toasted chopped nuts
1 cup flour
1 cup rolled oats
2 cups fresh blueberries, or other fruits chopped
1/2 cup melted butter
1/2 cup honey
1/2 cup brown sugar
1 tsp each: salt, baking powder, vanilla
1/2 tsp each: cloves, allspice

Combine all ingredients. Pour batter into a round or square oiled baking pan. Bake about 45 minutes, or until a fork comes out clean.

FRESH PLUM PUDDING

Our plums are ripe in August. We always harvest lots, if the raccoons don't get to them first. Oven at 350F

1 pound fresh plums
2 cups milk
2 TB flour
1/4 cup cold water
3 TB honey
1 tsp ginger powder
1/4 tsp nutmeg
2 beaten eggs
3/4 cup chopped walnuts

Halve plums and discard seeds. Arrange them in a 9 x 13 inch baking pan. Mix water and flour to form a paste. Add this paste to the milk. Warm it over low heat, stirring while it thickens. Add honey, ginger and nutmeg to the mix and warm while stirring, another five minutes. Remove from heat and cool five minutes, then add beaten eggs. Stir well and pour the mixture over the plums. Top with chopped walnuts. Bake 30 minutes or until the pudding is set.

BLUEBERRY MUFFINS

The blueberry family is rich in antioxidants. It includes our wild huckleberries, ripe at higher elevations in August and September. They are small but delicious, and great in muffins.   Oven at 400F

1-1/2 cups flour
1/2 cup rolled oats
1 cup apple juice
2 eggs, beaten

1/2 stick butter, melted
1/2 tsp each: salt, cinnamon, nutmeg, ginger
2 tsp baking soda
1 to 2 cups fresh or frozen blueberries

Oil the muffin tins with a little of the butter. Mix all the ingredients, gently adding berries at the end so they stay whole. Fill cups 2/3 full. Bake 17 minutes, longer for giant muffins.

SUMMER FRUIT DUMPLINGS
Oven at 350F

    Filling:
4 cups chopped plums, peaches, apricots, pears or nectarines
    Dough:
2 cups flour
1 tsp baking powder
1/2 tsp salt
1/2 stick melted butter
3/4 cups milk
    Sauce:
1 cup water
1 cup sugar
2 TB molasses
1/2 stick melted butter
1 tsp cinnamon
1/4 tsp nutmeg
1 tsp vanilla
    Topping:
Fresh whipped cream

Mix the dough ingredients and form dough into a ball with floured hands, then roll it out into 5 inch rounds. On one side of each round place some filling, then fold over and pinch the edges closed. In a large baking pan, mix the sauce ingredients.

Drop the fruit filled dumplings into the sauce and cover pan with foil. Bake 35 minutes. Serve warm or cold with whipped cream on top.

BLACKBERRY COBBLER

Cobble this one together in five minutes. Pick wild blackberries from early August. Great with blueberries, raspberries or Marion berries or use a mix of berries or berries with other fruits. Oven at 375F

    Filling:
1 TB butter
4 to 6 cups fresh or frozen blackberries
3 TB flour
1/3 cup sugar or to taste
1/2 tsp salt
    Crust:
2 cups flour
2 eggs
1 cup milk
1 tsp each: salt, baking powder, sugar
    Topping:
Whipped cream

Butter the baking dish, fill with berries and sprinkle them with flour, sugar and salt. In a bowl, mix the crust ingredients, flatten and shape to cover the berries. Bake 30 minutes or until crusts is a light brown.

LIN AND LYN'S SUBLIME FRUIT TART

My sister got this from our cousin Linda and it's now one of her stand-bys. Lynda makes several crusts at once and freezes them. Use almond paste or Nutella under fruit. A clear glaze seals in moisture, adds sweetness.

Crust:
1 stick of butter at room temperature
1 cup flour
1/4 cup powdered sugar
1/4 cup chopped walnuts

With ingredients in a pie tin or tart pan, use hands to form dough and spread it, then make a pretty top edge. Bake about 15 minutes or until it starts to turn golden. Let it cool.

Filling:
Thin some almond paste with a little water so it spreads. Or use a food processor or blender to make a "butter" of any nuts, to which you add just enough canola oil to allow them to blend. Spread a thin layer of nut paste in the bottom of the cooled crust. Slice soft fruits and lay them in a pretty pattern atop the base. In August, I use quartered figs from our tree and wild blackberries.

To hold the filling together, cook about a cup of fruit with two teaspoons of cornstarch, about 5 minutes. Pour this over the uncooked fruit laid in the crust. Or use thinned apricot jam or other fruit glaze to seal the top and make it glisten. Chill until time to eat it.

To make a strawberry tart, smash and simmer two cups fresh berries with 1 TB cornstarch until mixture thickens. Arrange two cups of fresh sliced berries in the cooled crust, then pour the cooked mixture over this.

Fall Fruit Pleasures

BEST BAKED APPLES
Oven at 350F

Halve and core 4 crisp apples, such as Fuji or Braeburn. Lay them in a baking dish, cut side up. Make a syrup of 2 cups cider, 1/4 cup brown sugar, 1/4 cup honey, 1 tsp cinnamon, pinch of salt. Heap apple centers with a mix of raisins, dried apricots, cloves and a dash of nutmeg and spread more filling around them. Pour syrup over and around apples. Cover with foil, bake 30 minutes, cool 20 minutes.

POACHED PEARS

This easy, healthful dessert for fall is pretty enough to share with guests.

2 perfectly ripe pears, cored and peeled
1/2 cup apple juice
1/2 cup white wine (or more juice)
1 TB honey
1/4 tsp each: ginger, coriander, cinnamon
1/8 tsp each: salt, nutmeg

Prepare pears, cut them in half the long way. In a wide pan, warm juice, honey, lemon, spices and salt. Mix well.

Lay four pear halves face down in the warm liquid, cover and simmer 15 minutes. Serve warm or chilled, with or without a scoop of ice cream.

CORVALLIS CARROT CAKE (takes 24-hours)

The overnight soaking of the moist ingredients gives this cake a rich flavor and fine texture. You just have to plan ahead.

4 large carrots, grated
1/2 cup honey
1-1/2 cup water
1 cup raisins
2 TB melted butter
1 tsp each: cinnamon, cloves
1/2 tsp each: salt, nutmeg
1 cup chopped walnuts
1-1/2 cup whole wheat flour
1 cup white flour

In a saucepan, combine carrots, honey, water, raisins, butter, spices, salt. Simmer together five minutes, cool and refrigerate overnight. The next day, set oven at 350F, then add nuts and flours, and mix well. Bake in a square or round 8-inch pan, about one hour or until a fork comes out clean. Frosting is optional.

FALL BLACKBERRY APPLESAUCE

Freeze some wild blackberries in zip lock bags so you can make this treat in late fall or winter.

6 medium apples
1 cup fresh or frozen blackberries or other berries
3 TB honey or to taste
1/2 cup water

Core, peel and cut up apples. In a covered, simmer apples on low heat until they are soft. Remove from heat and drain off water. Add honey and blackberries and stir just a little, so both gold and the berry colors remain separated. Serve warm or cold.

SUPERB APPLE PIE

A great apple pie is a bit of a project. It's best to handle or work pastry as little as you can, so it stays crumbly. This pie is tasty with a cup of blackberries in the filling, for a truly gorgeous color and taste. Oven at 350F

    Crust for one 9" top and one bottom:
2 cups flour
1/2 tsp salt
1 TB sugar
2/3 cup butter at room temperature
3 TB milk
    Filling for one pie:
4 cups peeled apple slices
1/2 stick butter, cut up into half inch bits
2 TB flour
3/4 cup sugar
2 tsp cinnamon
1 egg beaten with 1 TB water

For the double crust, in a bowl, mix flour salt and sugar then, with a large fork or pastry cutter, cut in the soft butter. Add milk, and a bit more milk if needed. Shape with hands and then let it rest 30 minutes. (You can also freeze dough at this point.) Press half the dough into the pie pan.

Fill shell with apple slices until they form a rounded hill. They will cook down. Distribute butter, sprinkle in berries then flour (so juices thicken up). Add sugar and cinnamon on top. Now roll out the remaining crust to about 1/8" thick and lay it over the top, using excess to make a pretty edge. For the egg wash or glaze, beat the egg with 1 TB water, and brush this over the whole top crust so it bakes to a beautiful glossy brown. Make some holes with a knife for steam to escape. Bake one hour or until the color is perfect.

ENGLISH APPLE CRUMBLE

This dessert is similar to an apple pie but a lot simpler to make. Oven at 350F

    Bottom:
Spread about 1/2 cup canola oil on the bottom of the baking pan. Sprinkle on 1/2 cup flour.
    Filling:
6 tart apples, cored, peeled and chopped
1 cup berries, or other fruit cut small
1/2 cup raisins or other dry fruit, cut small
1/2 cup sugar
1 tsp each: cinnamon and ginger
1/2 tsp nutmeg
    Topping:
1/2 cup flour
3/4 cup old fashioned oats (crisper crust that quick oats)
1/2 cup sugar
1/4 cup chopped walnuts
1/2 cup melted butter

Lay fruit on the oil and flour bottom, in a deep baking dish. Mix topping, using oiled hands, and crumble it on top. Bake about 50 minutes, until fruit is soft and crust is lightly browned.

MARGY'S FILBERT COOKIES

This recipe originated with Margy Buchanan, a Corvallis filbert grower. In some places, filberts are called hazelnuts. Oven at 350F

1 cup butter
1 cup sugar
2 cups flour
1 tsp vanilla
1/2 tsp salt
1-1/2 cup roasted filberts, ground

Cream butter and sugar together. Mix in other ingredients. Roll out like a piecrust and cut round or other shapes. Lay them on a cookie sheet, nicely spaced. Bake ten minutes. Remove from oven but leave them on the cookie sheet until they cool, so they don't break. They get better if kept a couple of days before eating, and they freeze well.

BERRY PUMPKIN BREAD

Since the berries are ripe before the winter squash, use berries frozen when they are their best. Any berry works. Oven at 350F

1 cup cooked pumpkin or winter squash
1 cup frozen blueberries or huckleberries
1/2 cup buttermilk
4 TB soft butter
2 eggs
1 cup chopped walnuts
2 cups flour
1/2 cup corn meal
1/2 cup sugar

1 tsp each: salt, baking powder, baking soda
1/2 tsp each: cinnamon, nutmeg, allspice

In a large bowl, mix first five moist ingredients. Add dry ingredients, mix until smooth. Bake in oiled loaf pan about one hour. Cool 20 minutes before removing from loaf pan.

FRUIT SPICE CAKE

If you use canned fruit, omit the fruit cooking step and use one cup each of apples or applesauce, and pears.
Oven at 350F

1 medium apple
1 medium pear
1/2 stick butter (1/4 cup)
1 cup whole wheat flour
1-1/2 cup white flour
1 tsp each: baking soda, cinnamon, ginger
1/2 tsp each: salt, nutmeg, allspice
1 cup sugar
1/4 cup molasses
2 beaten eggs
2 cups buttermilk
Garnish: 1 cup yogurt or sour cream, with honey

Melt the butter in a fry pan and, over low heat. In the butter, cook chopped fruit until soft. In a large bowl, mix all dry ingredients, then add cooked fruit, molasses, eggs and buttermilk. Mix well. Pour all of this batter into an oiled 8 x 13 baking pan. Bake 45 minutes or until a knife comes out clean. Serve warm, topped with a dollop of yogurt or sour cream mixed with honey.

FRESH PUMPKIN PIE

Pumpkin pie is so popular at our house that Joe asks for it instead of a cake on his birthday. I like to double the recipe and make two pies at once. Or, just make filling and call it pudding -- equally tasty and great for breakfast. This pie is excellent with canned pumpkin, or any meaty winter squash.

   Single piecrust:
1/2 stick butter
1/4 cup canola oil
1/2 tsp salt
1 cup white flour
1/2 cup whole-wheat flour
1/4 cup water
   Filling or pudding:
2 cups home cooked pumpkin
1 cup whole milk, or half and half
1/2 cup brown sugar
2 large eggs, beaten
2 tsp cinnamon
1 tsp ginger
1/2 tsp each: nutmeg, cloves, salt

Bake or microwave the whole squash until it's soft. Cool, peel and remove innards. Save the extra for soup or stew, in a few days. While squash bakes, make the piecrust. Melt the butter, add oil, salt and flour. With a fork, mix well, slowly adding water and keep gathering any crumbs into the ball.

Drop half the dough into the center of a pie tin and press it into the bottom. Make thick snakes of the remaining dough by rolling it between your hands. Then press these in around the sides, leaving enough to form a pretty pinched top edge.

Now back to the filling. Cut up and mash two cups of the soft squash or pumpkin. Or start with a 13- ounce can of puree. Add other filling ingredients and puree. This is where a wand mixer is handy. Pour filling into the pie shell. Any extra can be baked in an ovenproof bowl as pumpkin pudding. Bake the pie one hour, or until the filling is set.

Winter Fruits

WINTER FRUIT WITH YOGURT

Make this easy dish the night before and enjoy it for breakfast, with some whole grain toast.

2 cups whole milk plain yogurt
1/4 cup warm honey
2 cups total dry fruit – raisins, apricots, cranberries, etc.,
1/4 tsp salt
1/2 cup chopped nuts

Cut up large fruits. Mix ingredients, except nuts, and set aside so dry fruit can absorb moisture. Add nuts just before serving, so they stay crunchy. Serve chilled or at room temperature. Make it a dessert, with Margy's filbert cookies.

WINTER SMOOTHIE

2 cups yogurt, plain or flavored
1 cup frozen berries
2 cups apple juice
1 tsp vanilla
1/2 tsp nutmeg
Honey to taste

Whiz all together in a blender and drink chilled or at room temperature.

WINTER FRUIT SALAD

Cut up one fresh fruit – banana, orange, apple or pear. Add one cup frozen berries and one cup canned fruit. Dress with yogurt and warm honey.

APPLE SOUR CREAM TART

Similar to apple pie, the creaminess and the crumble topping distinguish this dessert. Oven at 400F

Pastry for a 9-inch shell (see Pumpkin Pie)
Filling:
2 cups diced tart apples, like granny smith
1 cup sour cream or plain yogurt
1/3 cup honey
2 TB flour
1 tsp vanilla
1/2 tsp cinnamon
1/4 tsp salt

Topping:
1 egg
1/2 cup brown sugar
1/3 cup flour
1/4 cup soft butter
1/4 tsp nutmeg

Peel and slice apples. Mix other filling ingredients and fold apples in. Pour all of this into the pastry shell. Bake 25 minutes. While it's baking, mix the topping ingredients into a crumble. At 25 minutes, remove the pie and sprinkle topping on it. Bake 20 minutes more.

APPLESAUCE SPICE CAKE

For the applesauce, you can substitute canned pears or fresh fruit. Oven at 350F

1 cup wheat flour
1-1/2 cup white flour
1 cup brown sugar, loosely packed
1 cup chopped walnuts
1-1/2 tsp each: vanilla, cinnamon, ginger
1 tsp baking soda
1/2 tsp each: nutmeg, allspice, salt
1-1/2 cup applesauce
1/2 up honey
1/4 cup melted butter or mild oil
2 eggs, beaten
1 cup buttermilk

In a large bowl, first mix dry ingredients, then add the rest and mix all together. Pour into an oiled baking pan or muffing tins. Bake muffins 15 minutes, cake 45 minutes or until a fork poked in comes out clean. Serve warm, topped with sour cream or honey and yogurt. I like the muffins for breakfast, with soft cream cheese.

APPLE AND PEAR CRISP

Thanks to our cousin Linda Hamer in Salem for this one. Oven at 350F

    Filling:
3 pears, firm and juicy
3 tart apples
1/2 cup dry cranberries
1/4 cup fresh apple juice
1/2 tsp each: orange peel zest, lemon peel zest, nutmeg, cinnamon
1/2 cup sugar
1/4 cup flour
    Topping:
1 cup white flour
1 cup brown sugar
1 cup oatmeal
1 stick butter, chopped
1/2 tsp salt

Peel, core and chop fruits. Mix with other filling ingredients and divide into ramekins or individual bowls. Mix all topping ingredients and divide on top of fruit in the bowls, forming a little heap that will cook down. Bake 45 minutes or until the topping is light brown.

SUSTAINABLE OPTIONS

DON'T feel guilty if you fail on any of these measures. Doing even one makes a small and personal difference and helps you feel empowered in a complex world of food and drink.

NO BOTTLED WATER Tests show it is more often than not drawn from municipal water supplies or contains more toxins than our more highly regulated tap water. If you are concerned, at home, install a filter system or use tap water run through a pitcher style filter such as Brita. Carry your own re-used water bottle. Americans trash 8 million plastic water bottles each DAY. World wide, plastic waste is a huge problem, polluting all the world's oceans and getting into seafood and other beings.

BUY ORGANIC and you reduce pesticide exposure in your home by 90 percent (unless you are using poisons in your yard). Oregon consumed 40 million pounds of herbicides and pesticide in 2007. Promote healthy land and agriculture.

READ LABELS and you soon become aware that many so-called "natural" products turn out to contain surprising ingredients. Many factory farmed organics with a pretty farm pictured on the package may be produced at an industrial scale and are highly processed before being shipped from very far away, so don't make good sense. To avoid GMO, look for labels that tell you it's not there. Assume that without this information some GMO ingredients were used. At least until labeling laws change.

BUY LOCAL when you can, and you minimize the average 1500 miles American food travels from farm to you. Support sustainable farmers near home. Keep them working and learning and keep your money in your own community.

BUT BULK FOODS They average half the cost of the same item in cans, bottles and boxes, and save all that wasted packaging. For items you must buy packaged, choose the largest size package you can use up, instead of more small ones.

GROCERY BAGS are a problem. Paper uses trees. Plastic uses petroleum. No plastic bag is cost effective to recycle. If you use them, reuse them. Cloth and fiber bags, on the other hand, can last for years and are easy to launder.

GOOD WINE AND BEER are made locally. Support your creative and industrious local maker. The Northwest has some of the best in the world, so why not reserve imports for rare occasions?

BABY FOODS are simple to prepare with a food processor, and then you really know what you're feeding your child. Use the tiny jars only when you are away from home, for sanitation. If you buy them, save and reuse the jars for homemade baby food or to store small things in the house or garage.

COOK instead of purchasing convenience foods that cost more and deliver less. Freeze extra for later. All it takes is shopping ahead and a little forethought.

CLOTH NAPKINS at home last many years. A dozen napkins laundered weekly add next to nothing to your cost of soap, water and energy. Use only the paper you truly need when eating out. Paper napkins alone add six billion pounds yearly to US landfills, and devour many trees.

PAPER TOWELS are great for small, greasy messes. For other clean-up chores use cloth. A handy bag of rags, and laundering, is a far greener option. Recycle old tee shirts, linens etc. into cleaning rags. In public restrooms, take only as much as you really need, not five feet of paper to dry hands.

FOOD STORAGE is safest in ceramic or glass. When you store in plastic, wait until food is cool to put it into the container. Warmer food absorbs more chemicals from plastic. Toss out any plastic with a "7" in the recycle triangle – it could be made of almost anything in the category of "other." Clear glass saucers as covers let you see the leftovers in bowls. Use masking tape to label leftovers, so you don't forget what you have and let it rot.

FOOD CONSERVATION Freeze some for later, save scraps for stock, leftovers for lunches or soup making. Use old bread for bread pudding or duck food. About 15 percent of the meat Americans buy ends up as garbage -- a sad waste of animal life. Freeze leftover meat, add to it to veggies and noodles and make soup. Turn leftovers into dog food.

COMPOST FOOD WASTE Garbage disposals add excess food nutrients to waste water, nutrients that promote overgrowth of micro-organisms that disrupt water ecosystems. Keep a bag or bucket in the freezer for every bit of food you can't use at the moment. Later, sort it and make stock. Compost food waste -- or at least the soft stuff. If you must use a disposal, run the cold water, not the hot, and save both energy and pipe clogs.

COMPOST enriches the garden, and feeds all your outdoor plants from tulips to fir trees. Keep a covered bin near the sink then bury, scatter or use a serious compost system to get it back into the earth as worm food, where it's a valuable resource.

DISHWASHERS made in the past 20 years don't require pre-rinsing. Pop in the dirty dishes, seal the door to keep ants out, then run it only when full. Doing these things saves an average of 20 gallons per load.

MICROWAVE OVENS use one-fifth to one-third the energy of an electric oven or burner. For best efficiency, keep the inside nice and clean. And cover all food. This keeps the inside of the oven clean but, more important, it keeps the gases from plastic that lines the oven away from your food.

STOVES work best when the pot fits the burner. Water boils faster, by about 15 percent, when you cover the pot to keep heat in.

OVENS never need more than five or ten minutes of preheating. Food continues to cook in residual heat if you turn off the oven ten minutes before it's time to remove the project. If you have an hour's worth of baking to do, might as well bake several things at the same time.

TOASTER OVENS are ideal for small jobs and small families.

PRESSURE COOKERS quickly tenderize dry beans, peas and tough meats. Pressure cook bones in water with a little vinegar for an hour and you extract calcium and other important nutrients for stock. At high altitudes where water boils at a lower temperature, they make a huge difference by allowing water to get hotter. Modern stainless steel pressure cookers are totally safe.

REFRIGERATORS work day and night and are the kitchen's energy hogs. Open the door and the chill slips out, heat goes in. Ice-makers and side-by-side doors suck up extra power. Avoid locating a fridge in a warm or sunny spot.

BE NEIGHBORLY Borrow instead of making a special trip to the store. Buy bulk as a group and divide up that 100-pound purchase. Go in together and buy half a grass-fed beef to freeze. Then celebrate with a barbecue. Share a ride to pick berries together. Do potlucks and exchange recipes. Trade excess garden goodies.

CULTIVATE CREATIVE FRUGALITY
What's good for the budget is also good for the environment.

RELEVANT READING

Allen, Darina, Ballymaloe Cooking School Cookbook, Pelican Publishing, 2002. The director of an Irish culinary academy shares recipes, techniques and creative ideas that once only her students could access, in this encyclopedic guide to great eating, based on food from a climate like ours.

Araldo, Josephine and Robert Reynolds, From a Breton Garden, Addison-Wesley Publishing, 1990, takes you to rural France with a woman whose ancestors loved their local foods. She went to Paris for Cordon Bleu training and brings that refinement to her simple recipes for garden-based meals.

Ash, John, From the Earth to the Table. A top Napa Valley chef uses California's regional bounty in simple but sophisticated dishes.

Bowden, Jonny, PhD, The 150 Healthiest Foods on Earth, Fairwinds, 2007. "The surprising and unbiased truth about what you should eat and why," this book will entertain the biochemist in you with loads of facts about how foods and human physiology interact, explaining not only what to eat but presenting solid recent research evidence for why.

Bradley, Susan, Pacific Northwest Palate, Addison Wesley, 1989. With a Seattle-focus, this book explores delightful ways to utilize regional ingredients through the seasons. The author founded the Northwest Culinary Academy. Her deep familiarity with what's produced in our region and her clear explications mark her as a gifted teacher.

Brody, Jane, Good Food Gourmet, Bantam, 1992, is by a science and food writer for the New York Times, who loves to cook for and with friends and offers a fine collection of easy, low-fat, real food recipes.

Carucci, Linda, Cooking School Secrets for Real World Cooks, 2005. Offers "tips, techniques, shortcuts, hints plus 100 sure-fire recipes." And it's fun to read.

Fallon, Sally, Nourishing Traditions, New Trends, 1999, is an encyclopedic re-visiting of how we eat that challenges some politically correct misconceptions and corrects the errors of recent dietary notions. Fallon provides hard science to back up her ideas about the nutrition we need for total health and the benefits of some neglected foods and fermentation products. It includes lots of good recipes and directions for making tasty new and very ancient foods and dishes.

Fernandez-Armesto, Felipe, Near a Thousand Tables, Free Press, 2002, is a wise and highly entertaining history of eating, beginning with our Neolithic ancestors. Journey through the odd and irrational ways we have nourished our bodies and created our cultures of food from the dawn of civilization, through the ups and downs of various empires, and into the present. The author teaches history at Oxford and the University of London.

Fisher, M.F.K., With Bold Knife and Fork, G.P.Putnam's Sons, 1968, and her many other delightfully chatty books about food and cooking are true classics and fun to read. Her recollections of sensuous and humorous encounters with memorable meals take us back to an era worth knowing.

Galton, Jean, The Pacific Northwest. Williams Sonoma's New American Cooking, 2000. The series is beautifully illustrated and provides clear steps for creating elegant meals inspired by top regional chefs.

Geise, Judie, Judie Geise's New Northwest Kitchen, Madrona Publishers, 1987, has lots of European-inspired easy gourmet recipes and wine suggestions from the northwest's top restaurants, reflecting that period's Northwest culinary revolution.

Gibbons, Euell, Stalking the Wild Asparagus, and his other books about foraging changed the way many looked at nature, helping us appreciate the edible bounty all around us. He lived in the northeast, but many of the featured plants grow here.

Hazan, Marcella, Marcella Cucina, Harper Collins, 1997, invites you to come into an Italian kitchen with a very likeable, and spirited cook, to see exactly how she works with food to produce simple, delicious, traditional dishes.

Hill, Tony, Herbs and Spices, the spice lover's guide, John Wiley & Son, 2004, explores tasty items from Ajuain to Zeodary, and includes formulas for making your own traditional and special purpose spice blends.

Hyman, Mark, MD, The Ultra Metabolism Cookbook, Scribner, 2007, is about eating to lose weight and get healthier. The recipes are tasty and of wide variety. Ideal for someone who wants to make some lifestyle changes to feel good again.

Ingle, S. and S. Kramis, Northwest Bounty, Sasquatch Press, 1999, features regional ingredients in from-scratch family favorites, from many traditions and in all categories from soup to dessert.

Jaffrey, Madhur, World Vegetarian, 1999, has more than 650 meatless recipes from around the world by a true master of exciting international taste, using vegetables, fruit, beans, nuts, grains, dairy, and a glorious assortment of spices, many in tasty and healthful ways we rarely experience.

Katzen, Mollie, The Enchanted Broccoli Forest, Ten Speed Press, 1982, is a great classic hippie vegetarian cookbook by the spirited author of The Moosewood Cookbook, filled with basic food information and inspired recipes hand lettered by Mollie herself.

Kavasch, E.B., Native Harvests, from Dover Publications (no date), features Native American wild foods and recipes from the entire country, with some good sections on using and preparing plants, meats and seafoods of our area in truly traditional ways.

Kingsolver, Barbara, et al. Animal, Vegetable, Miracle, a year of food life, HarperCollins, 2007. Follow one family's experience living from their own land for a year, the ultimate in choosing local food. "We fed ourselves, organically and pretty splendidly we thought, on about fifty cents per family member, per meal," belying accusations that the movement is elitist.

Mcnamee, Thomas, Alice Waters and Chez Panisse: The Romantic, Impractical, Often Eccentric, Ultimately Brilliant Making of a Food Revolution, Penguin Press, 2007. In this gossipy authorized bio, follow Alice through the decades. An impulsive young girl and sensual lover of French food finds her iron will, flawless taste, rich friendships and grand vision to grow a little Berkeley restaurant into an international mecca of fresh local cuisine.

Meyers, Perla, Fresh From the Garden, Clarkson Potter Publishers, 1996. A Connecticut gardener grows a variety of vegetables and offers simple delicious recipes from all over the world, for using them.

Nims, Cynthia, Wild Mushrooms, Westwinds Press, 2004, and Stone Fruits, 2003, and others in the Homegrown Cookbook series are gorgeously illustrated with Don Barnett's watercolors. These narrow-focus, broadly conceived books artfully explore a number of food groups, one by one.

Peterson, James, Cooking, Ten Speed Press, 2007, is a big beautiful book with 600 recipes and 1500 photos, offering the reader a remarkably complete kitchen education. In this ultimate how-to for today's home cook, Peterson starts with the basics and includes hundreds of step-by-step photos.

Peterson, James, Simply Salmon, Stewart, Tabori and Chang, 2001, is the definitive guide to preparing the Northwest's favorite fish in dozens of ways. Clear directions and insightful explanations enrich the text.

Pisegna, David, Food for all Seasons, Savory recipes from the Pacific Northwest, Chronicle Books, 1990. Ahead of his time, Pisegna offers uncomplicated but elegant cooking based on our region's seasons and local food products. Photos by Dick Busher inspire beautiful presentation.

Planck, Nina, Real Food, What to Eat and Why, Bloomsbury Publishing, 2006. Delightfully readable and packed with great research and absorbing facts, this book, like Sally Fallon's, will make you rethink most of the myths that permeate our current thinking about what's healthy to eat.

Pollan, Michael, The Omnivore's Dilemma: a natural history of four meals, Penguin, 2000. A UC Berkeley professor examines in delightful prose our confusing and faddish food choices, be they industrial and fast food, organic or what we forage or grow ourselves. Acclaimed author Pollan has also written The Botany of Desire: a plant's eye view of the world, and In Defense of Food: an eater's manifesto.

Polvay, Marina, All Along the Danube, Hippocrene Books, 2000. Easy and interesting traditional foods from Germany, Austria, Slovakia, Hungary, Croatia and Serbia, made from ingredients we produce in the Northwest.

Schreiber, Cory, Wildwood, Cooking from the Source in the Pacific Northwest, Ten Speed Press, 2000. Building on a family history of great Northwest food, Schreiber opened Wildwood Restaurant in Portland and won the James Beard Award as Best Chef: Pacific Northwest. He knows the territory, and loves finding the best stuff. Elegant eats, fine historical and food photos.

Taggart, Dan and Kathleen, Northwest Food and Wine, Sasquatch Books, 1998, is perhaps the best wine lover's northwest harvest recipe collection, starting each section with a group of fine regional wines and offering instructions for elegant but not complex dishes to serve with them.

Traunfeld, Jerry, The Herb Farm Cookbook, Scribner, 2000, includes over 200 recipes, gorgeous herb paintings, plus a complete guide to handling and cooking with fresh herbs to bring out their subtle and refined flavors. His popular garden and Herb Farm Restaurant are east of Seattle.

Vollstedt, Maryana, The Big Book of Breakfast, Chronicle Books, 2003, is filled with great recipes and directions for serious comfort food for mornings or any time of day, by a respected Eugene food author.

Waters, Alice, The Art of Simple Food, Chez Panisse Vegetables, Chez Panisse Fruit, and her many other good books are wonderful openings into Waters' French-inspired ideas about creating refined, incredibly delicious food from the freshest of simple, natural ingredients in season.

Windle-Humphrey, Sylvia, A Matter of Taste, Macmillan, 1965, described as "the definitive seasoning book", it was one of the best of its time, (along with Elizabeth David) on how and why to use herbs, spices and flavorings to bring out the best in any food, a skill sorely needed by American and English home makers back then -- and for most of us now.

QUIPS AND QUOTES

"The discovery of a new dish does more for human happiness than the discovery of a new star."
    Jean Anthelme Brillat-Savarin

"It is inconceivable how hearty I ate and how comfortably I felt myself after it."
    James Boswell

"There is no love sincerer than the love of food."
    George Bernard Shaw

"Vegetables are a pleasure to buy and clean and prepare, and then cook them and serve forth. I love their colors, odors and the feel of them... I look better, at least in my own eyes, and I feel and think better, if I eat a lot of them."
    M.F.K. Fisher

"No place on Earth, with the exception of Paris, has done as much to influence my professional life as my native Oregon."
    James Beard

"Any fool can make a roast. It takes a genius to know what to do with leftovers."
    Josephine Araldo

"What's at stake in our eating choices is not only our own and our children's health but the health of the environment that sustains life on earth."
    Michael Pollan

"To consume processed food is to hand over total control of one's diet to absolutely unknown other people. Trust, in these circumstances, is fragile."
    Margaret Visser

"My bioregion is the small patch of Gaia I have come to know and love, and that I hope to protect."
    Connie Barlow

"I show them a barrow full of rich soil...saying This is where it all starts, in the good earth, and if you don't have clean fertile soil you won't have good food or pure water... denatured soil doesn't have the essential minerals and trace elements we need in our food."
    Darina Allen

"Local vegetables...retain their personality, their connection to terroir and to the farmer. Isn't that the ultimate luxury?"
    Chef Adoni Luis Aduriz

"Regional cuisine continues to be a meaningful term for home cooks because of its reliance on letting the season dictate what should be cooked, which often happens to be the products grown or produced nearby."
    Michael Ruhlman

"Eat foods that spoil. But eat them before they do."
    Nina Planck

"Let's grow everything we eat, and what we can't grow, we'll at least buy from local organic sources, including the nearest farmers' market. And let's continue that for an entire year, doing what we can to reduce the miles traveled and the oil consumed by the food served on our table."
    Barbara Kingsolver

"The joy of watching new shoots and buds appear is incalculable; the joy of transforming the food we have grown ourselves is immeasurable. Where would the cook be without a garden?"
Sheridan Rogers

"We are growing more of our own food...foods not addicted to petroleum. It's just a start...I'm a big proponent of gardens, not lawns."
Winona LaDuke, activist, Ojibwe tribe

"Frankly, I think it takes a little bit of being crazy to make a difference in the world."
Erin Brokovich

"Rational exploitation of nature has to stop short of despoilation. We have been turning too much of the planet into too much food: wasting resources, endangering species. Fussiness and 'foodism' are methods of self-preservation for society, against the deleterious effects of the industrial era: the glut of the cheap, the degradation of the environment, the wreckage of taste."
Felipe Fernandez-Armesto

"Throw out as much non-organic processed food as you can afford to. Avoid anything genetically modified, artificially created or raised with hormones. Don't eat ingredients you can't pronounce."
Robyn O'Brien

"Millions of Americans seek a more fulfilling, just and sustainable way of life. This America is out of the limelight, yet it is where I see hope for both America and the world."
Da-le Jiajun Wen, activist Chinese scholar

"Given our current knowledge of the planet's capacity, we now realize that producing enough food is not enough – it must be done sustainably."
　David R. Huggins, soil scientist

"I eat when I'm hungry, eat what I'm hungry for, and don't eat too much. What I like more than anything is easy – six minutes in the microwave for a baked potato."
　Joe Henderson, fitness and running author

"Finding the time, energy and means to prepare nutritious meals for oneself and one's children poses a real challenge, especially as the temptation to opt for convenience foods is very great... Fast foods are a terrible trap that, in the long run, leads to diminished vitality and, hence, even greater restrictions on one's time, energy and budget – not to mention the tragedy of serious disease."
　Sally Fallon

"Any intelligent fool can make things bigger, more complex and more violent. It takes a touch of genius – and a lot of courage – to move in the opposite direction."
　B.F. Schumacher

"The real local food is in your refrigerator right now. Don't drive all over looking for some special ingredients. Make a fine meal out of what you've got."
　Frank Ratti, in conversation

"You can't make good food without good products, and you can't get good products when they are out of season."
　Daniel Rose, Chef at SPRING in Paris

"In the long run, I don't want to rely too heavily on others to produce my food. I want to have an ace in the hole, so to speak. Plus, I really enjoy gardening, and it is something I want to pass on to my kids."
  Robert Rapier, on line

"To cook with exuberance, awareness and joyousness, we must open our hearts to the world of dew-covered gardens, alpine light, fiery sunsets, languid bays, and fragrant forests... The steps we take today will shape not just the cuisine of the Northwest, but its ecological future, the delicate balance between humans and nature."
  David Pisegna

Made in United States
Troutdale, OR
09/22/2023